MONTANA WILDERNESS

DISCOVERING THE HERITAGE

By Steve Woodruff and
Don Schwennesen

Photographs by Carl Davaz

Published by The Missoulian
in cooperation with The Lowell Press, Kansas City

MONTANA WILDERNESS
DISCOVERING THE HERITAGE

was written by Steve Woodruff and Don Schwennesen,
photographed and designed by Carl Davaz,
with map design by Kirk M. Johnson,
photocomposed in Times Roman,
and printed on 80-pound Warren's Flokote Enamel,
a neutral pH paper with an expected 300-year
library storage life as determined by the
Council of Library Resources of the
American Library Association
by The Lowell Press,
115 East 31st Street, P. O. Box 1877, Kansas City, Missouri 64141

Library of Congress Cataloging in Publication Data
Woodruff, Steve.
Montana wilderness.
Includes index.
1. Wilderness areas—Montana.   I. Schwennesen, Don.
II. Davaz, Carl.   III. Title.
QH76.5.M9W66 1984   333.78'2'09786   84-15433
ISBN 0-913504-88-2
ISBN 0-913504-89-0 (pbk.)

First Edition
Copyright © 1984 by The Missoulian, a division of Lee Enterprises, Inc.

Printed in the United States of America
by The Lowell Press of Kansas City, Missouri

Rays from the rising sun tint the rocky face of the Chinese Wall, winding northward from Cliff Mountain, foreground, in the Bob Marshall Wilderness. On the cover, a solitary explorer climbs a ragged ridge overlooking the Bob Marshall's White River drainage.

CONTENTS

Where marshes meet mountains, Swan Lake reflects wispy summer clouds in Red Rock Lakes Wilderness. The Centennial Mountains, in the background, rise nearly 4,000 feet from the valley floor. Such areas of solitude and beauty shape the lives of all Montanans.

FOREWORD

Wilderness is a way of preserving some small part of the natural grandeur that once seemed endless

MONTANANS REGARD THEMSELVES as kin of Lewis and Clark, those first recorders of accurate knowledge of the West's flora, fauna, and native inhabitants. Their expedition of discovery looms large in the state's history, for it was here the explorers spent more time and covered more miles than in any other part of their journey. As they followed the wild Missouri to its headwaters, they described for Thomas Jefferson the vast land abundant in forests, animals, grassy plains, and clear waters.

Here was the place where earth, sky, and water came together in bountiful reaches, a land so generous and giving that taking became expectation. The fur traders took the beaver, the hunters the bison, the miners the minerals, the lumbermen the timber, the plowmen the grasses. Every product of nature was treated as though it were inexhaustible. In a world of such abundance, the erosion and abuse were slow to show and easy to bypass.

Today only 10 percent of Montana's great heritage remains as Lewis and Clark first saw it, and of that less than one-third has been placed by Congress in the wilderness system. The remainder, all federal land, is open to projected assignment for roads, timber, and mining.

In spite of the disappearing natural resources, Montanans are still the spiritual sons and daughters of Jefferson's explorers. They are attached to the frontier and the wilderness not for sentimental reasons, but because of deep-rooted values about the land.

My own experience comes from years of watching the political and economic pressures that have been put upon the environment. I learned from Lee Metcalf that there is a connection between the way land is managed and the well-being of the public. During my childhood, my

Striking 10,000-foot-high mountains dominate the Spanish Peaks area in the Lee Metcalf Wilderness. More than a century after Lewis and Clark trekked through Montana, modern explorers are again discovering the beauty and importance of the state's wild lands.

father and I roamed all his favorite spots in western Montana—his fishing grounds, his birding marshes, his vistas for fresh perspectives. But for over 40 years, I was away. And when, in 1979, I again had time for scouting the outdoors, I found how changed it was.

I had taken trusting comfort from 20 years of legislation aimed at better stewardship of public lands. But now I view the changes of one lifetime: the clearcuts, the bulldozed roads, the gravel washed for gold at the foot of a waterfall. If legislation is not enough, if research and polls that endorse protection are not enough, then I must, since I care, work in every additional way possible to see that Montana's few remaining natural areas are saved.

There is no time for dwelling on the long-gone days of the twenties, when I could drift through alleys of fragrant evergreen in my family's Maxwell or trek shank's mare to a picnic site whose season was marked by trilliums, wild roses, or elderberry. Today I pursue my relationship to the land in meetings called to affirm the value of balanced natural systems. The people with whom I meet are lawyers, bankers, professors, foresters, engineers, accountants, and land planners. We seek to protect ecosystems that depend, as we do, upon secure habitat, clean air, and fresh water.

The opportunity for such protection is limited. It remains in only a few areas—areas for which the wilderness system provides the highest likelihood of success.

Whatever future there is for wilderness must be seized immediately. We could preserve the heritage of a shared world that so enhances the quality of life and maintain the valuable balance of flora and fauna built over millions of years. Why should we not preserve for succeeding generations some small part of the natural grandeur that once seemed so endless? Why should we not open our minds?

DONNA METCALF

INTRODUCTION

A source of inspiration and awe, wilderness is a force that shapes the lives of all Montanans

Montana, one of the last frontiers in America, is a place where vast expanses of land remain relatively untouched by more than a century of growth and development. Towering mountains guard pockets of wilderness that have never been fully explored. Rolling prairies hold traces of bison and the Indians who once roamed free. Even the state's largest cities are built near the edge of wild territory where people and grizzly bears share narrow forest trails.

Wilderness is the heart of Montana. The state contains more than 3.4 million acres of congressionally designated wilderness areas and millions of additional acres of equally wild country. With a total population of 818,000—about one-half the number of people living in the city of Philadelphia—Montana has nearly 4 acres of wilderness for every man, woman, and child in the state. The Big Sky Country has roughly 14 percent of the 23 million acres of wilderness in the continental United States. Only neighboring Idaho, with 3.9 million acres, and distant Alaska, with 56 million acres, have more wilderness.

At one time, any tract of undeveloped land could be described as wilderness. Passage of the Wilderness Act of 1964 changed the term to mean a specific area set aside by Congress for preservation in its natural state. Increasingly, wilderness is becoming a word almost synonymous with conflict. Loggers are fighting for the wilderness timber they need to supply their sawmills, and miners are struggling to keep the areas open for mineral exploration. Environmentalists are battling to save some of the last remaining wild country in America for future generations. "We're fighting for the last scraps," says environmental activist Joan Montagne of Bozeman.

Mount Harding in the Mission Mountains Tribal Wilderness seems small beneath the famed Big Sky. Wild wide-open spaces are an important part of life in Montana, but growth and development are forcing hard choices about the future of wilderness.

Changing times have brought increasing pressures to bear on the state's wild lands. Natural resources are becoming more valuable, and the number of people competing for them increases daily. Bulldozers and chainsaws are threatening even the most remote and pristine corners of the state. But until the competition for wilderness is settled, Montana's major industries must struggle through tough economic times while many of the natural resources they need are held in limbo.

Wilderness is an economic issue that affects to some degree the pocketbooks of all Montanans. Valuable natural resources allocated to wilderness cannot be used to make lumber. Mountains that are managed to preserve natural qualities cannot accommodate ski areas or resorts. Wilderness locks away, theoretically forever, the natural gas or oil that might be found deep underground. In a developing region where the economy is fueled largely by the wood products and mining industries, where jobs are often scarce, and where people have a long tradition of exploiting natural resources, the arguments against wilderness can be compelling.

"Large numbers of the people who belong to the environmental groups that advocate wilderness do not depend on natural resources to make a living, as we do in Montana," says Gary Langley of the Montana Mining Association.

Yet wilderness has an economic value of its own as an attraction for tourists and recreationists. It is hard to say how much of the state's $300 million tourist business stems from wilderness, but many of the people who visit Montana each year come to see the unspoiled natural beauty, the wide-open spaces, and the plentiful wildlife found in its wildest places. It is relatively easy to count the board feet of timber in a forest and to calculate its value as two-by-four lumber. Figuring the monetary value of the same area as wilderness is much more difficult, making dollar-for-dollar comparisons impossible.

A black bear cub in the Great Bear Wilderness, right, watches from the safety of a tree while a group of people passes by. Preservation of wild lands is important to the many types of wildlife that depend on secure habitat for survival. Above, dark ridges and a bright sky frame A Peak in the Cabinet Mountains, an area epitomizing the clash between wilderness and economics: the Cabinet Mountains provide a home for a dwindling population of grizzly bears, and the wilderness also contains one of the richest mineral deposits in America.

Wilderness is not simply a matter of money. It is a moral issue, too. It represents the long-overdue recognition that humans do not have the right to disrupt every last acre of earth. Wilderness preservation is a means of making sure that at least some of nature's beauty survives. Someone once asked pioneering conservationist Bob Marshall how much wilderness America really needs. "How many Brahms symphonies do we really need?" Marshall asked in reply.

To people deeply involved in the preservation movement, discussions about wilderness economics seem absurd. Gaylord Nelson, chairman of the Wilderness Society, tries to imagine wilderness philosophers like Marshall and Aldo Leopold talking about the value of untrammeled territory. "Marshall and Leopold probably wouldn't have spent 5 minutes arguing the economics of wilderness," he says. "There's just a sense that some of nature's work ought to be preserved."

Wildland preservation raises scientific and social questions as well. For example, do we need areas controlled by natural processes against which to measure the changes of civilization? And how can the public gain the most benefit from its lands?

People are not the only ones affected by wilderness preservation. Some species of wildlife cannot live in close association with humans. Animals and birds like the grizzly bear, the Rocky Mountain wolf, and the trumpeter swan need large expanses of wild country in which to live.

Simply defining wilderness often becomes a matter of dispute. Should wilderness be only the highest rock-and-ice summits of mountains, or should it include a wide range of areas representing every ecosystem in the country?

The clash of economic, moral, and other questions makes the wilderness issue a difficult one to settle. Myths and misunderstandings further confuse matters. Wilderness sometimes is characterized as a playground for the wealthy, the elite, and the out-of-state tourists. People opposed to wilderness preservation complain that it upsets the multiple-use philosophy under which most public lands are managed. Environmentalists, mistrustful of commodity-oriented government agencies, contend that wilderness restrictions are the only means of protecting fragile lands.

In fact, the state's wilderness users comprise a broad cross section of people, most of whom live in Montana. Wilderness is a form of multiple use: it prohibits logging, mining, and motorized vehicle use but protects the land for wildlife, water quality, scientific research, and recreation.

And the Wilderness Act is only one of several laws designed to preserve public lands.

Perhaps the most common misconception is that once an area is designated as wilderness, its future is secure. Examples found throughout Montana's wilderness areas prove that designation is just the first step toward preservation. Wilderness is a resource that requires thoughtful management to prevent its accidental destruction.

Wilderness is an important part of life for Montanans. Their wild surroundings, visible from their homes, ranches, and highways, are a source of inspiration and awe. Those who enter the wilderness find that the complexities of workaday life seem to fade, and simple things take on greater importance. Few people can traverse a canyon carved by ancient glaciers or contemplate the earthly power needed to build the Rocky Mountains without gaining a truer perspective on their own lives. "You get to thinking that you're pretty important," says wilderness ranger Mac Brandon of Red Lodge. "Then you look at a place like this, and you know you're not."

Regardless of whether they value it as a place of untapped opportunity or as a rare sample of purity spared from the forces of progress, wilderness shapes the lives and livelihoods of all who live in the nation's fourth-largest state. "Montanans have a visceral understanding that our last, best wild places are not only our weather makers, watersheds, and home for the great creatures of the continent, but they also are part of each Montanan individually," Congressman Pat Williams says.

It is not just the presence of wilderness, but what it does to people that sets Montana apart from most of America, says Daniel Kemmis, speaker of the state House of Representatives. In an insightful 1983 essay on Montana values and politics, Kemmis recognizes the lure of the wilds as the reason most people make the state their home: "If you ask people—especially those who clearly remember their arrival here—why they are here and not somewhere else, you hear time and again the story of feeling crowded, oppressed, and alienated elsewhere, the need to be able to get into the open country, to experience its power, to identify oneself in relation to that kind of open land."

Gov. Ted Schwinden says that securing a reasonable amount of wilderness is essential to preserving Montanans' way of life. "Those resources, once lost, are captured only in prose, art, photographs, or memory," he says.

As intricate and fragile as ice crystals on a trailside puddle, wilderness inspires complex questions about preservation of public lands.

"Some of us who live here don't appreciate what we have here," Schwinden adds. He recalls a conversation with an out-of-state newspaper reporter visiting Montana for the first time who said, "I didn't believe there were places like this left in the world."

Never has it been more important for people to discover Montana's wilderness heritage. Decisions made in the coming years will partly determine how much of Montana's frontier character survives. The allocation and protection of wilderness resources will help set the pace for economic development for generations to come. All Montanans, all Americans will have a stake in the issue and a voice in its outcome.

People who explore the resources and issues of existing wilderness areas will find it easier to make informed decisions about these and other wild lands. This book is a beginning in the search for answers and understanding about Montana's wilderness.

The following pages offer a journey through the state's 15 designated wilderness areas. Each chapter has a different theme focusing on a specific wilderness issue. The issues range from economics to wildlife, from what constitutes wilderness to how best to manage it. Every area is unique, but the issues affecting each are common to all wildernesses. The chapters are like pieces of a puzzle that fit together to provide a portrait of one of Montana's most precious resources.

Chapter 1

ABSAROKA-BEARTOOTH

A lofty bastion of wildness surrounded by an encroaching world of human pressures

From the top of Montana, the wilderness seems boundless. Mountains stretch out in every direction, their peaks of jumbled granite cutting the horizon into a sawtoothed pattern of rock and snow. Flowing from the mountainsides are long plateaus, tundra-covered tables that run for miles before breaking into fields of boulders that spill steeply into distant valleys. Here, in the heart of the Absaroka-Beartooth Wilderness, Granite Peak, Montana's highest mountain, thrusts 12,799 feet into a cobalt blue sky. There is a vastness to this mountain, this place. But there are limits to the Absaroka-Beartooth, and they are steadily closing in. Even mighty Granite, the wildest of Montana mountains, is under pressure from the world outside.

The Absaroka-Beartooth, a sprawling, 920,400-acre wilderness in the Gallatin and Custer national forests between Billings and Yellowstone National Park, is a land of natural paradox. It is one of the most inaccessible and inhospitable places in the state. But it is also an area of captivating beauty.

In the Beartooth Mountains, on the eastern side of the wilderness, 28 peaks rise to 12,000 feet or higher. The mountains are described in part by their names: Tempest, Froze-to-Death, Thunder. The high-altitude Beartooth plateaus form the largest single expanse of land above 10,000 feet in the United States. The Absaroka Range, in the western portion of the wilderness, contains less-rugged mountains—steep ridges flanked by grassy meadows and timbered canyons. A harsh, subarctic climate dominates the wilderness. Winter, with its howling winds and heavy snows, comes and goes with little regard for the calendar. Temperatures can plummet 40° Fahrenheit in a matter of hours.

Its beauty as rugged as the landscape, Froze-to-Death Plateau bathes in the warm glow of sunset beneath the summits of Mount Tempest, left on the horizon, and Granite Peak. Nature defends its lofty reaches with formidable terrain and often violent weather.

Summer is a fleeting season interrupted by almost daily thunderstorms that hammer the mountains and plateaus.

Yet the Absaroka-Beartooth has a beauty that is as subtle as tiny phlox blossoms clinging to a rocky ledge and as spectacular as a waterfall crashing hundreds of feet into a crystalline lake. This is a land of water. Glaciers and perennial snowfields feed more than 950 gemlike lakes—almost all in the Beartooth Mountains—laced together by a network of rushing creeks and rivers. The entire wilderness is a watershed of unsurpassed quality for the Yellowstone River.

For all its harsh landscape, it is a fragile place where nature's tenuous grip on rock and shallow soil is easily broken.

The Beartooths are built on a foundation of Precambrian gneisses and schists, believed to be some of the world's oldest rocks. This foundation was covered by thousands of feet of Paleozoic and Mesozoic sedimentary rock, then uplifted nearly 70 million years ago by the same geologic forces that built the Rocky Mountains. Glaciers and weather scoured away the covering of sedimentary rocks, unearthing the flat, uplifted Precambrian foundation that forms today's plateaus. The high mountain peaks are islands of sedimentary rock that survived eons of erosion. The Absarokas are made of softer sedimentary rock that weathered into gentler, more rounded mountains.

Glaciers still dot the rugged Absaroka-Beartooth, but they are small remnants of the icy shield that once capped the region. Other reminders of the distant icy past include rugged alpine cirques and deep, U-shaped valleys.

Elusive bands of bighorn sheep inhabit the plateaus, while mountain goats claim the alpine cliffs. Deer and elk summer in the wilderness, and many of the lower creek drainages have small populations of moose. The wilderness is considered good habitat for the threatened grizzly bear, although its numbers are few. Black bears make their home here as

1

well. Some people suspect that there may be an occasional Rocky Mountain wolf, an endangered species, but the evidence is limited to a few scattered tracks. Other wildlife includes wolverines, mountain lions, coyotes, bobcats, martens, marmots, and a host of small rodents. Birds include blue and ruffed grouse in the timbered canyons and bald and golden eagles in the skies above the plateaus and ridges.

About one-fourth of the lakes contain fish. Only a few waters, mostly in the Slough Creek Drainage, have native populations of trout; the rest have been stocked. Cutthroat and brook trout are the most common species, but rainbow and golden trout, arctic grayling, and whitefish are also present.

The Crow Indians cherished this region, sharing with it their name for their own tribe, Absaroka. They named the rugged mountains after fanglike Beartooth Mountain, on the southeastern edge of today's wilderness. Historians believe that ancient hunters began venturing into the Absaroka-Beartooth 9,000 years ago. Crow Indians climbed here to hunt the once-plentiful bighorn sheep. The U.S. Forest Service set aside portions of the region as the Beartooth and Absaroka primitive areas in 1932, and Congress named it a formal wilderness area in 1978.

The Absaroka-Beartooth has always been a place for man to visit, not to live. Through most of time, this wild land has remained inviolate.

But now humans, in their insatiable pursuit of pleasure and wealth, are increasingly encroaching on the wilderness. Many people equate wilderness designation by Congress with salvation of a natural area because the Wilderness Act prevents most kinds of development. But wilderness protection does not eliminate all threats to wild lands. As with many other wilderness areas throughout the nation, the outside world is leaning hard on the Absaroka-Beartooth.

The marks of man are clear throughout the Absaroka-Beartooth. Glacier and Mystic lakes are both dammed reservoirs. The Absarokas are still healing after decades of overgrazing by domestic sheep. And timber stands throughout the wilderness are growing decadent and vulnerable to pests and disease as a result of the overaggressive fire-suppression practices of the past.

The people who come here in search of climbable mountains, big trout, or simple solitude leave the most noticeable scars. The Absaroka-

Flowers cling tenaciously to rock on the seldom-visited southern flank of Granite Peak. Mountain goats, facing page, share their alpine domain with growing numbers of hikers.

Beartooth has become a national playground, ranking as the fourth-most-visited wilderness in America. All the visitors combined spent a total of 392,000 days in the Absaroka-Beartooth in 1983. Only the Boundary Waters Canoe Area in Minnesota, the John Muir Wilderness in California, and the Alpine Lakes Wilderness in Washington draw more visitors than the Absaroka-Beartooth. So many people come here each year that pollution from human waste has become an alarming problem.

Backpackers scrounging for firewood have created what foresters call a "human browse line" around many of the lakes. In alpine areas, a campfire can consume in minutes a tree that took centuries to grow. Several such fires by backcountry travelers can seriously disrupt a fragile natural system. Wherever man goes, he leaves his fire rings—blackened rocks circling a bed of charcoal—to mar otherwise pristine scenery.

Other problems include campsites denuded of vegetation and fragile soils compacted by informal trails through meadows. Caches of trash can be found in even the most remote corners, where supposedly only the most experienced and knowledgeable hikers go. Climbing to the top of Granite Peak, Forest Service rangers recently gathered and packed out sacks of soiled toilet paper. Even the first men to ascend the peak left their initials chiseled in the rocky summit.

Some wilderness visitors inflict plainly malicious damage, like carving initials on trees or discarding garbage on a lakeshore. But the most common vandalism can be attributed to simple carelessness, like that of a troop of hatchet-wielding Boy Scouts camped sloppily on the shores of Rainbow Lake.

Fishermen are among the worst offenders, leaving their Styrofoam bait containers everywhere and scattering fish entrails in the clear lakes, where the cold water slows decomposition. The most trampled and abused areas in the wilderness are around lakes containing fish.

Modern roads and trails make it easy for people to penetrate the Absaroka-Beartooth. Major roads provide access to the wilderness from the four compass points of Billings, Big Timber, Livingston, and Cooke City. People living along the eastern approaches to the wilderness steer clear of Road 307 between Red Lodge and Roscoe on Friday nights because of the heavy traffic from Billings. If they drive their cars fast enough, people can leave work in Montana's biggest city in the late afternoon and be in the wilderness before dark.

The Forest Service estimates that about 70 percent of the people

Dominated by Mount Cowan, the Absaroka Range stretches to south central Montana's jagged horizon. Winter loosens its hold slowly in this land of extremes. Long after summer arrives in the lower elevations, the high country remains blanketed by snow.

who venture into the Absaroka-Beartooth live in nearby Montana cities. Located conveniently close to Yellowstone Park, the wilderness has also become a major attraction for out-of-state tourists. Articles in popular magazines have lured tourists by accurately billing the area as one of America's premier wilderness areas.

Once they reach the wilderness boundary, visitors will find 32 major trailheads and more than 700 miles of maintained trails. But the rugged topography often concentrates recreation use in narrow corridors. Predictably, most of the backpackers congregate on weekends and holidays, within 10 miles of major trailheads. The most heavily used areas include the East and West Rosebud canyons and the popular Cooke City-to-Alpine trail. Thompson, Knox, and Rainbow lakes frequently support small cities of tents during the summer. In the fall, hunters swarm into the Slough Creek, Hellroaring, West Boulder, and Buffalo Fork drainages. Wilderness rangers have found that few people stray farther than a quarter-mile off developed trails. For the relatively few hikers who do leave the trails, who sweat and struggle to reach the

hundreds of isolated lakes and mountains that have no trails leading to them, the reward is solitude.

Concerned about damage caused by the growing number of people who visit the Absaroka-Beartooth, the Forest Service encourages wilderness users to treat the land with more respect. It has banned camping within 200 feet of lakes and 150 feet of streams. Wilderness rangers patrol the heavily used areas, enforcing regulations and preaching no-trace camping practices. They take the work seriously. "When someone hurts this place, it's like they were hurting me," says Blase DiLulo, a charismatic ranger who has spent a lifetime working in and around the Absaroka-Beartooth. The rangers are making progress toward protection, too. Wild strawberries and wildflowers are now struggling to take hold in campfire rings that were dug up and reclaimed a decade ago. Yet, as DiLulo says, "Everybody's got to do their part, or we're going to lose it."

Recreationists are not the only threat to this great area. Modern-day prospectors equipped with bulldozers and drilling rigs are pressing their search for precious metals to the very fringes of the wilderness.

The boundaries of the Absaroka-Beartooth were drawn to avoid conflict over resources like minerals and timber. Most of the timber in the wilderness area is either too stunted or too remote to be considered worth logging. The area also seems largely devoid of minerals that interest miners, and the wilderness has little potential for producing oil or gas.

However, just across the Absaroka-Beartooth's northern boundary is the Stillwater Complex, an amazingly rich belt of minerals running 26 miles between the Rosebud and Boulder rivers. The Stillwater Complex contains the largest chromite reserve in the United States, one of the nation's largest reserves of nickel and copper, and a huge zone of platinum and palladium that is still being explored. The chromite is a high-iron ore that is imported to the United States for less than it would cost to mine it in Montana. And mining nickel and copper ores in the Stillwater Complex is unlikely soon because those ores are relatively low-grade.

But the platinum, a precious metal worth roughly the same as gold, is a different story. Mining claims for most of the complex are controlled

Indian paintbrush and other wildflowers add splashes of vibrant color to lush alpine meadows. Such delicate details help soften the Absaroka-Beartooth's rough edges.

5

A butterfly finds an ugly perch on boots abandoned in a fire ring, right. Rangers like Blase DiLulo, above, work to heal scars on the land.

by the Stillwater Mining Company, a consortium of the Anaconda Minerals Company, the Manville Corporation, and the Chevron Resources Company. Although the consortium is still exploring its find, mining appears likely. The mining would take place outside the Absaroka-Beartooth boundary, but it could disturb life inside the wilderness through noise and air pollution. Bill Cunningham of the Helena-based Montana Wilderness Association worries, too, that large mining operations could bring an influx of people to surrounding communities—people who could increase the human pressures on the Absaroka-Beartooth. "There certainly is the potential for adverse impacts," Cunningham says. "It depends on how many people this brings."

A 2-mile hike to Passage Falls, near Livingston on the western side of the area, offers a look at yet another threat facing all of America's wilderness areas: political pressure.

When the Absaroka-Beartooth was established, it surrounded a 50-acre enclave of private land, an old homestead patented in the 1920s near the falls on Passage Creek. The homestead was recently subdivided into 33 parcels, and some of the owners want to build summer homes on their land. To do that, they need a road on which to haul building materials. Wilderness laws do not restrict development of private land, but the landowners were prevented from building their cabins because

A road being built near Passage Falls, above, proves wilderness laws are an obstacle to development, not a guarantee of protection.

the law forbids building roads across wilderness. Congress solved the problem in 1983 by redrawing the Absaroka-Beartooth boundary to take a 27-acre corridor near Passage Creek out of the wilderness. Work is proceeding on the road.

Although 27 acres is but a small fraction of the expansive Absaroka-Beartooth, the loss points to a weak spot in the wilderness-protection law: whatever Congress does, it can quickly undo.

Yet, like the unknown effect of nearby mining, political pressures remain mostly a potential threat. Recent efforts to open a snowmobile trail through the heart of the Absaroka-Beartooth, for example, did not get far. To date, wilderness has survived more major battles in Congress than it has lost. But who knows whether future generations of politicians will place as much value on an area like the Absaroka-Beartooth?

The potential exists for man to damage seriously, if not destroy, the wilderness qualities of this area. The people who come here to fish, hike, or probe the earth for riches may ultimately decide whether the potential becomes real. But for now, Granite Peak, the vast windswept plateaus, and the deep, dark canyons survive largely intact. Man and his activities have threatened, but not conquered, the wilderness. The Absaroka-Beartooth remains a bastion of wildness surrounded by a world of human pressures.

Chapter 2

RATTLESNAKE

A wilderness on the brink of civilization, a place where simple ideals mix with complex realities

THE LIGHTS OF MISSOULA flicker in the distance when twilight settles over the Rattlesnake Wilderness. Neon signs twinkle, and car headlights weave like fireflies in the gathering darkness. The bright city contrasts sharply with the timbered ridges and rocky peaks of the Rattlesnake Mountains, where sunset casts a delicate pink glow. The only movement here is the wind, which gusts and swirls around deep cirques. After dawn, when the city fades into the haze of the valley below, daylight reveals more surprises: forests scarred by clearcut logging, glacial lakes held captive by earthen dams, and gravel roads that penetrate fragile alpine basins.

The 33,000-acre Rattlesnake is a wilderness perched on the brink of civilization. Wild, but not pristine, the area inspires one of the most fundamental questions in wildland preservation: what constitutes wilderness?

The Rattlesnake's winding ridges and secluded valleys rise from the backyard of Montana's third-largest community. The area lies within walking distance of Missoula, and downtown pedestrians need only look beyond the rooftops to catch a glimpse of its mountain peaks.

No other wilderness area in the West lies so close to a sprawling city. Yet the Rattlesnake holds scattered pockets of remarkable wildness, hidden valleys tucked beyond the reach of all but the most adventurous hikers. Fewer than 1,000 people hike into the wilderness each year, a fraction of the number attracted to Montana's better-known wilderness areas. Most Rattlesnake visitors head for the picturesque campsites and sometimes-good fishing at Twin, Farmers, and Little lakes. Relatively few hikers seek the lush basins and small valleys surrounding 8,620-foot

Fresh snow covers trees growing on the steep slope-of Rattlesnake Ridge. Winter brings solitude to the Rattlesnake along with deep snow and frigid temperatures. Regardless of the season, people seldom enter the area's northernmost basins, in the distance.

McLeod Peak, a former vision-quest site for Salish Indians.

The Rattlesnake contains a collection of compact, lake-filled basins, each nestled between sheer headwalls and sloping forests. From the southern end of the wilderness, a knife-edged ridge arcs north past Stuart and Mosquito peaks, winding ever higher toward McLeod Peak, the tallest and northernmost mountain in the Rattlesnake. Bowl-like Grant Creek Basin hangs from the gentler timbered western slope of the ridge. To the east, the ridge top falls off sharply into high cliffs, cirques, and sparsely timbered basins. The area's northern boundary joins the Flathead Indian Reservation only a short distance from the Mission Mountains Tribal Wilderness. The area immediately north of the Rattlesnake is a tribal sacred area closed to non-Indians. The Rattlesnake National Recreation Area, covering the lower elevations of the watershed, is a narrow natural buffer between the city and the southern boundary of the wilderness.

Grizzly bears, the living symbol of wild Montana, travel through the Rattlesnake's upper reaches. The area forms the southernmost portion of the great bears' range in the northern Rocky Mountain ecosystem, although the resident grizzly population is scarce, at best. The Rattlesnake also is home to bald eagles, goshawks, ptarmigan, and nearly 100 other species of birds. Small groups of mountain goats still winter on the cliffs above Rattlesnake and Grant creeks, although their numbers have dwindled at the hands of hunters and poachers. Biologists are trying to restore goat populations by transplanting animals captured on the National Bison Range near Moiese. White-tailed and mule deer range throughout the forested areas along with a few elk. Many of the alpine lakes are stocked with rainbow, eastern brook, cutthroat, and Dolly Varden trout. Despite the area's name, rattlesnakes keep to the lower elevations and have never been reported in the wilderness.

Rimming the U-shaped Rattlesnake Valley, the wilderness is the headwaters of Rattlesnake Creek and Missoula's municipal watershed. More than 50 small creeks collect from springs, melting snowbanks, and clear lakes, bringing to Rattlesnake Creek water of uncommon purity. The parasite *Giardia lamblia* has infected portions of the creek close to town, but the wilderness waters remain clean and clear. The Rattlesnake's importance as a watershed has long shielded it from the widespread logging, subdivision, and home-building that tamed similar nearby mountain valleys.

Although the area has few valuable minerals, it includes features of possible importance to geologists. Like most of Montana, the Rattlesnake was covered by glaciers during a series of ice ages that began nearly 60,000 years ago. Other glaciated areas of North America were largely reworked by each succeeding covering of ice, but the Rattlesnake was scoured by progressively smaller glaciers that left untouched, in the higher elevations, the geologic marks of past ages. The glaciers produced the Rattlesnake's distinctive headwalls, cirque basins, and lateral moraines. The mountains here are built predominantly of quartzite, argillite, limestone, and siltite. The rocks that form the platelike base of the Rattlesnake were the bed of an ancient sea about 1.5 billion years ago. Geologists believe that the rocks formed perhaps 25 miles to the southwest, drifting over the eons to their present location.

On a map, the Rattlesnake boundaries are defined sharply. In the mountains themselves, the boundaries become less clear. Only Rattlesnake Creek and a few open fields separate the first one-half mile of the main access trail from scattered suburban homes. The trail is an old road that passes rusted wire fences, abandoned homesteads, and a concrete bridge before reaching the wilderness. Nearly 80 percent of the people who visit the Rattlesnake stay within 3 miles of the main trailhead, never venturing beyond the national recreation area. Many people have no idea where the wilderness begins and ends.

Few Montanans questioned the need to preserve the Rattlesnake, but many fought over whether it qualifies as wilderness. Joe Mussulman, a University of Montana professor who works as a Forest Service ranger in the Rattlesnake, was among the skeptics. "It's a wilderness legally but not environmentally," he says. Mussulman knows the area as well as anyone, having explored it for nearly three decades. He led the initial public drive for protection of the Rattlesnake but fought against its wilderness designation. "Wilderness," he says, "is something I know I'm in when I can't find a trail." Bob Marshall, the man who founded America's wilderness-preservation movement one-half century ago, described wilderness similarly, calling it a place that "preserves as nearly as possible the primitive environment."

Yet wilderness, like beauty, is in the eye of the beholder. "Some people, when they're driving through on the interstate, perceive all of Montana to be a wilderness," says Lance Olsen, a Montana psychologist active in wilderness issues. Other people contend that the only true wildernesses are the rock-and-ice summits of the highest mountains, an argument that seems to confuse the words *primitive* and *pure*.

Thurman Trosper, a retired forester and former president of the Wilderness Society, says the issue of wilderness purity is a smoke screen the Forest Service and others use to limit the size and number of wilderness areas. "If you have to pick an area that's absolutely pure, then no area will qualify," he says.

The Rattlesnake, for example, is primitive but hardly pure. Portions of the area overlook a community of 65,000 people. Red lights blink incessantly atop television and radio transmission towers on nearby TV Mountain, and Boeing 727s roar over its ridges on their approach to Missoula's Johnson-Bell Field. Inside the wilderness boundary, the area is marked by man's handiwork. Humans made their first permanent intrusions in 1911, when workmen and mule teams began building rock-and-timber dams on eight of the Rattlesnake lakes.

The Montana Power Company, which once owned the city water system, bought and protected for decades more than 20,000 acres of the watershed as a means of guarding its investment in the water business. But in the 1950s, the company began logging its land. Loggers pushed a road deep into the area, reaching inside what would later become the wilderness boundary, to clearcut large tracts of the Lake Creek and Wrangle Creek drainages. Although the logging stopped, partly because of public criticism and partly because the best timber had been harvested, the roads remained.

As nearby Missoula grew, the area became a handy recreational retreat for city residents, who used the rough, narrow road along Rattlesnake Creek as the avenue of easiest access. The increasing number of people brought litter, gouged trails, and erosion.

Montana Power closed the Rattlesnake to cars and trucks in 1970 out of concern for water quality. But the area remained open to motorcycles, which could quickly carry fishermen to the popular alpine lakes. Because careless riders used their motorcycles to scramble to the most fragile corners of the area, damage to the land continued.

Many people who came here sought escape from the clamor of the city and were offended by the noisy machines. Public concern about damage from motorcycles broadened into general community interest in proper management of the Rattlesnake's resources, and an organization called Friends of the Rattlesnake in 1971 began lobbying to protect the area. The group studied the many land-preservation statutes and strategies. Any number of laws might have worked, but only one, the federal Wilderness Act of 1964, would preserve the area's wild qualities and assure the elimination of motorcycles.

Although touched by human activity, the Rattlesnake is an example of the kind of place Congress had in mind when it established the national system of wildland protection. Recognizing that wilderness takes many forms, Congress tossed aside the dictionary and wrote its own definition of wilderness. It described wilderness as "an area where the earth and its community of life are untrammeled by man, where man himself is a visitor who does not remain."

Wilderness areas are places with recreational, scientific, educational, scenic, or historic importance. The Wilderness Act provides a marvelously elastic definition that recognizes simple ideals and complex realities. It uses words and phrases like *untrammeled, primeval character,* and *natural condition* but softens them with the words *generally, primarily,* and *substantially.*

Congress wields the act to protect a variety of areas for a variety of reasons. Wilderness can be a remote range of awe-inspiring peaks or a marshy nesting area for trumpeter swans. It might be a popular hiking area or a fragile ecosystem of scientific interest. America's wilderness areas range from mountains in Alaska where few men have ever traveled, to small forested tracts in Missouri where nature is slowly reclaiming old garbage dumps.

Wilderness areas are managed to protect natural conditions. Motor vehicles are barred, logging is outlawed, and buildings and other permanent structures are prohibited. Mineral exploration was allowed until the end of 1983; now mining is allowed only on existing valid mineral claims. Hunting, fishing, camping, and other forms of primitive recreation are allowed but sometimes restricted to prevent damage to wilderness resources. The regulations protect only public lands, although in cases like the Rattlesnake, private parcels are sometimes included inside wilderness boundaries in hopes that government agen-

A tent atop Murphy Peak commands an impressive nighttime view of Missoula. City dwellers live within walking distance of the Rattlesnake.

cies might later buy or trade for the lands.

Business and industry groups fought against wilderness designation for the Rattlesnake, calling an area that includes roads, clearcuts, and dams a distortion of the wilderness concept. But Friends of the Rattlesnake President Cass Chinske says man's imprint on nature should be viewed in proper perspective. "It all depends on the intensity," Chinske says. "Those dams up there are not real high impact. They are not real ugly. This road is not ugly. I've been in Glacier National Park and walked up trails just the same size."

Wilderness philosophers might never agree about what constitutes a truly wild area. In practice, the issue is a political one where wilderness becomes whatever Congress says it is.

For the Rattlesnake, wilderness may be a matter of law that eventually becomes a fact of nature. Man has undeniably touched this area. But, protected from development, the land now will be left to heal. Already, motorcycles have been banned from the wilderness and adjoining areas. The Forest Service is rapidly acquiring private lands inside the Rattlesnake so they, too, may be protected. Even in the Rattlesnake clearcuts, forests of rotting stumps are yielding to a new generation of trees, while the hard-packed roads are slowly disappearing beneath a carpet of weeds and wildflowers.

Chapter 3

CABINET MOUNTAINS

A mountainous land where natural treasures and monetary values balance precariously

THE HIGH SPUR RIDGES of the Cabinet Mountains drop gracefully away from the rocky peaks, then plunge into the long, deep fault valleys that bound the mountains east and west. Viewed down the length of the range, they seem from some vantage points to form a line of arching buttresses separating glaciated valleys that open like the entrances to alcoves along a cloister. According to local tradition, early French trappers viewed the shouldered ridges, with their regular openings, and saw the semblance of a tier of "cabinets" or chambers.

The sequestered chambers of the Cabinet Mountains Wilderness hold an array of riches: diamond lakes, pearly cascades, emerald rain forests, and a king's ransom in silver, copper, lead, and gold. The treasure rooms of the Cabinet Range were unlocked nearly a century ago, while Montana was still a frontier. Old mines border the wilderness, their names—the Snowshoe, the Gloria, the King, the Golden West, the Heidelberg—pages in local history. During the first two-thirds of this century, mines in and around the Cabinets produced more than 25,000 ounces of gold and 1 million ounces of silver. But as the surface veins gradually played out, the old miners were squeezed out, caught between the rock and the hard place of inflating production costs and a fixed federal gold price. Their labors unearthed but a fraction of the wealth beneath the Cabinets. Forgotten digs in the shadow of St. Paul Peak reveal that they passed over the blue-green outcrops of low-grade ore far up Rock Creek and Copper Gulch in the southwestern end of the range.

Today, a new generation of miners has returned to the Cabinets. Equipped with technology that can literally move mountains, they have discovered a thick seam of low-grade copper-silver ore that passes

An exploratory drill rig probes ASARCO mining claims at the base of St. Paul Peak in the heart of the mineral exploration area of the Cabinet Mountains Wilderness. The company hopes to mine deep underground, tunneling from a mile outside the wilderness.

beneath the southwestern Cabinet peaks like a swath of frosting between the layers of a cake. Mining geologists traced the ore zone from similar deposits to the northwest, just across the narrow Bull Valley in the West Cabinet Range, where a new ASARCO Incorporated underground mine in Lincoln County is already the largest silver producer in the nation. Processing as much total ore every 2 months as Lincoln County produced in 6 decades, the new mine extracts more than 40 million pounds of copper and 4.2 million ounces of silver a year. Exploration geologists say the deposits beneath the Cabinet wilderness are even richer, yet they will scarcely put a dent in the voracious appetite of a technological world hungry for metals.

In a region where the timber industry has held sway, mining adds a new dimension both to the wilderness debate and the local economic balance. Where past battles have turned on whether to harvest and manage roadless timberlands, mining claims may affect timbered or alpine lands. Access can disrupt wildlife, and a discovery may mean rapid community growth and competition for local skilled workers.

The Cabinets are stormy mountains with an elusive past. The most westerly of Montana's wilderness ranges, they are—at the 48th parallel—the first tall rib of the Rockies to catch the Pacific storms from the Cascades, more than 200 miles to the west. Often shrouded in clouds, they receive up to 110 inches of precipitation annually, much of it as winter snow. The alpine snowpack piles to 10 feet or more, and a summer visitor may sometimes spot in a tree overhead an old trapper's notch marking where a trap once rested on the crest of the winter snowpack. Huge old cedars, hemlocks, grand firs, and white pines cloak the lower valley bottoms. Tangled thickets of alder, mountain maple, and huckleberry climb the open sidehills and avalanche chutes.

The origin of the ore locked within the quartzite beneath the mountains is a mystery obscured by long ages in geologic time. The

Snowshoe Peak crowns the Cabinets, a wilderness where rocky crags tower above luxurious forests along such streams as Granite Creek.

bowels of these mountains were formed as a seabed, beginning perhaps 1.5 billion years ago, as primordial continents still barren of life were abraded by rain and snow into fine sands and silts that in turn swept away down nameless rivers to settle into seas that have passed into eternity. For nearly 1 billion years the seabed thickened, and the deep layers fused into quartzite under the intense pressure and heat of molten rock injected from the earth's core. Mineral veins followed by the early miners are evidence that plutonic forces infused the Cabinets with mineral lodes. But the deeper, low-grade deposits of strata-bound ore are more cryptic. At times the deeper strata may have lain beneath an arid basin in which inland seas periodically rose and evaporated. The receding seas may have concentrated dissolved minerals into rich brines that eventually became deposited in the quartzite layers known today as the Revett geological formation.

Thrust up along with the rest of the Rockies during the mountain-building period that began roughly 70 million years ago, the Cabinets were scoured during the Ice Age by glacial icepacks nearly as thick as the range is high. Yet even the glaciated alpine valleys remain broken by stairstep ledges, cliffs, and shelves that defied the age of ice.

The Cabinet Mountains Wilderness extends for 33 miles along the mountain crest, forming a 94,272-acre preserve that is generally from 4

Antlers still sheathed in summer velvet, a young mule deer moves silently among boulders of the high country it prefers. Shimmering Granite Lake, facing page, mirrors the towering summit of A Peak in the central Cabinets, the highest portion of the range.

to 7 miles wide. One of Montana's first wild areas, it was set aside as a Forest Service primitive area in 1935 and officially classified wilderness with the passage of the 1964 Wilderness Act. In elevation the Cabinets are not a lofty range, but they rise from the lowest corner of the state, towering more than a mile above the surrounding valleys. Snow-shoe Peak, in the midsection of the range is, at 8,712 feet, the highest summit. Mantled by Blackwell Glacier, it forms the backdrop for Leigh Lake, largest of the 85 lakes in the wilderness. Nearby 8,634-foot A Peak and 8,174-foot Bockman Peak are the only other mountains over 8,000 feet. The modest elevations belie the rugged splendor of the Cabinets. Sheer walls plunge more than 1,000 feet from crags such as St. Paul Peak, on the southern end of the range, and Snowshoe. About 25 spur trails climb the side valleys, typically ending at alpine lakes within 2 to 7 miles of the trailhead. A few lead to unmarked routes across the northern and central range, where steep scrambles ascend the tallest peaks. Hikers

outnumber horsemen nine-to-one in the Cabinets. Livestock forage is scarce. With relatively short trails ending in rugged, alpine terrain, the Cabinets offer few opportunities for the extended saddle tours most horsemen prefer.

Fishing is a major attraction for wilderness visitors. Most of the lakes support native cutthroat trout, but some offer rainbow and brook trout, first introduced in the early 1900s. Many lakes were originally barren. In 1970, a visitor survey found that 65 percent of the people using the Cabinets were local residents, and 67 percent were on day trips. Nearly two-thirds of all visitors journeyed to just five lakes along the eastern side of the range. Leigh Lake accounted for 28 percent of the visits; Geiger, Granite, Cedar, and Sky lakes attracted another 36 percent. In the winter of 1981-1982, a snowslide felled trees for about 300 yards on the lower end of Leigh Lake. Kootenai National Forest managers, who had been pondering how to reduce human impacts at the lake, decided to accept nature's solution to the problem and leave the windfall in place. "It kind of covered up a lot of the heavily used area," says Gary Morgan, forest staff officer for recreation and minerals. "It isn't all that easy to get to the lake anymore."

Moose, elk, and white-tailed and mule deer summer in the Cabinets. Mountain goats inhabit the range year-round, and bighorn sheep introduced in 1969 are flourishing around Berray Mountain, on the western wilderness boundary. Mountain lions and black bears are abundant; in 1983, grizzly researchers trapped 40 black bears before finally capturing a grizzly. Sightings of the rare woodland caribou, a relative of the arctic caribou, were reported in the southern Cabinets as recently as 1962. Rare sightings and reports of tracks north of the Cabinets have persisted since then. But this most endangered of all North American ungulates slips inexorably toward extinction and may already be gone from Montana, representing a notable management failure. There are no plans to reverse the situation. Managers say the caribou's large territorial needs make it difficult to protect. The animal also feeds largely on lichens in old-growth forests, a habit that puts it in direct conflict with timber production goals of liquidating old timber and raising younger trees.

The threatened grizzly bear may be headed for a similar fate in the Cabinets, but it is in the management spotlight today. Impacts of mining and other activities are often evaluated now in terms of the grizzly in areas such as the Cabinets where the great bear still survives. A creature

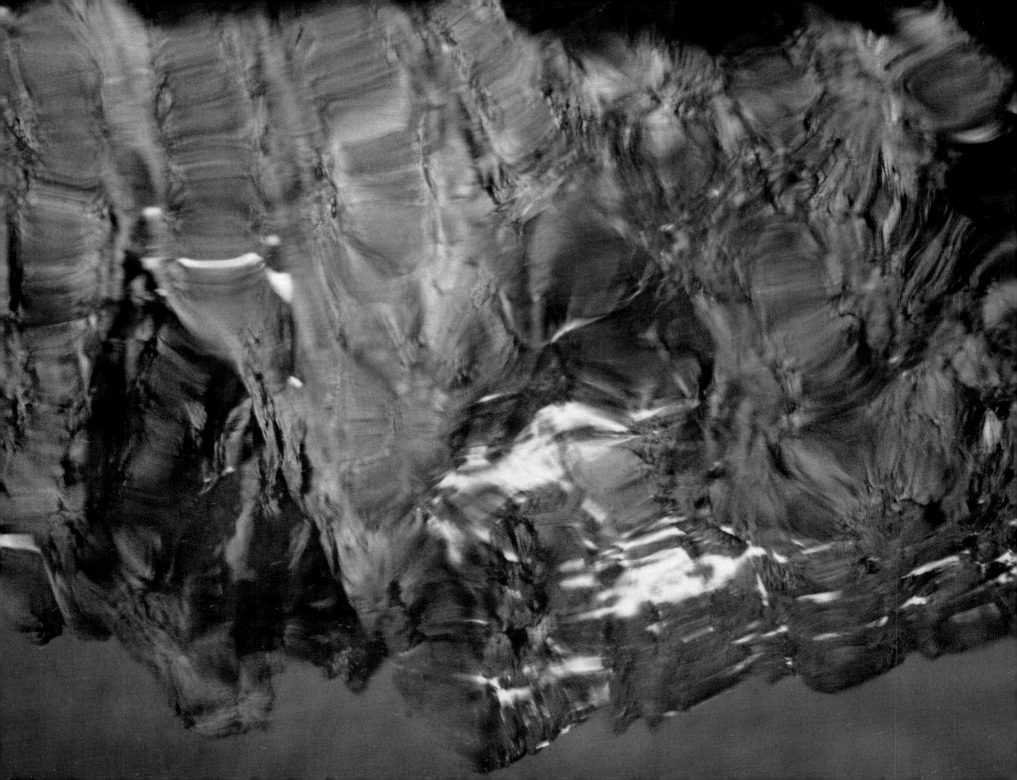

with large territorial needs, the grizzly is a threatened species protected under the Endangered Species Act. Managers often run a gauntlet of public criticism as they search for ways to satisfy conflicting laws that encourage mining but also mandate grizzly protection.

A decade ago, grizzlies and mountain goats were the major hunting attractions in the Cabinets. Now probably no more than a dozen grizzlies are left. Sightings are rare. The lone grizzly captured and fitted with a radio collar in 1983 was a 28-year-old female believed to be the oldest documented free-ranging grizzly on record. The Cabinet grizzlies face twin pressures: mining under the southwestern flank of the wilderness and possible development of a major ski resort on the southeastern edge. Great Northern Mountain, south of Libby, is the proposed site for the resort that some local residents believe will bolster the area's timber-dependent economy. Old mining claims at the mountain's base could become lodge and condominium sites. As development pressures close in on the southern Cabinets, wildlife managers struggle to understand the remnant grizzlies and their needs.

Few of the conflicts the managers face are as glaring as that between mining and wilderness. Many people are amazed that mining can occur within a wilderness. But the nine-year political battle leading to the 1964 Wilderness Act was a conflict that ended in compromise.

Miners had been given a free hand on public lands by the 1872 Mining Act. The spirit of the act was to promote mineral production for industrial growth. The act allowed prospectors to stake claims anywhere on the public domain and obtain outright ownership of their claims if they could prove the land would yield profitable minerals. Mining interests feared that wilderness legislation would diminish their favored status. They asserted, and still argue today, that minerals were the ultimate source of all material wealth. Many minerals were scarce, they added, and the nation did not have the luxury of ignoring important reserves within wild areas. Wilderness advocates, defending the genetic, scientific, and aesthetic wealth of wild lands, responded that most mineral deposits already had been found. Potential wilderness areas had been spared because they contained no significant minerals. Under the eventual compromise, wilderness boundaries were drawn to exclude known mineral deposits. Miners were granted 19 years to explore

High in Copper Gulch, a boulder on the slopes of St. Paul Peak bears the turquoise sheen of copper ore that outcrops nearby. Deeper ore known as bornite is steel blue.

wilderness areas and stake new claims. They also gave up the right to obtain surface ownership of wilderness claims. The implication was that any mining scars in wilderness areas ultimately would be reclaimed.

The Cabinet wilderness boundary reflects the compromise. Along the southwestern edge, most of the Rock Creek drainage lies outside the wilderness due to the old, yet still active Heidelberg Mine. The excluded arm of land penetrates deep into the mountains, and the wilderness corridor shrinks to one-half mile in width. One primitive road serves the mine, and a second climbs to 6,000 feet on the western flank of Chicago Peak, where timber was harvested up to the wilderness boundary in steep clearcuts two decades ago.

In 1979, ASARCO began drilling exploratory holes near Milwaukee Pass, a short walk from the end of the Chicago Peak Road, to extract rock samples from potential copper-silver deposits hundreds of feet below. The mining firm also unveiled a 4-year plan to drill about 100 similar holes on as many 20-acre claims near Chicago Peak, St. Paul Peak, and Milwaukee Pass. Drilling equipment was shuttled to the drillsites by helicopter under the watchful eyes of Forest Service managers and conservationists worried about the future of the wilderness. The 4-year drilling plan was reviewed by the Kootenai National Forest and the U.S. Fish and Wildlife Service, the agency charged with protecting threatened species such as the grizzly. Ultimately the plan was approved with dozens of stipulations restricting helicopter flight patterns, regulating use of drilling water from alpine lakes, limiting drilling seasons, and requiring special carpeting under motors and drill rigs to catch minor spills of fuel or lubricants. To provide extra living space for grizzlies disturbed by the drilling, Kootenai rangers closed four roads, canceled one timber sale, and postponed three others.

The plan was still challenged as inadequate by the Sierra Club Legal Defense Fund, Defenders of Wildlife, and a local group known as the Western Sanders County Involved Citizens. But their lawsuit was dismissed, both a federal district court and an appeals court having concluded that the federal agencies had adequately protected the grizzly based on available information. Students from the University of Montana Wilderness Institute monitored the drilling work in 1980, and Forest Service monitors continued thereafter. In 1981, the Forest Service expanded its grizzly work by reviewing the cumulative impact of all types of activity in and near the wilderness.

The study divided the Cabinets and surrounding forests into

A drilling foreman examines a rock sample from the last exploratory hole drilled in the wilderness, on a U.S. Borax claim. Time ran out for new exploration at the end of 1983.

hypothetical bear habitat units, each covering about 100 square miles and containing sufficient habitat to support one female bear with cubs. The study projected that as many as 30 square miles of any unit could be temporarily disturbed without harming resident bears. But even that limit was pressed in 1982, when a second mining firm entered the Cabinet minerals race. U.S. Borax staked claims on both sides of ASARCO and unveiled drilling plans that would have cut one bear unit to 60 square miles. To accommodate both firms, the Forest Service closed more roads and required both firms to work in the same drainages at the same time.

At the end of 1983, time ran out for wilderness claim-staking. Plastic ribbons still flutter from trees marking the corners of the wilderness claims, but few traces of the drilling can be found. In 1984, while the Forest Service was still evaluating Cabinet mineral samples to judge their potential, ASARCO announced its corporate verdict. The firm unveiled plans for a major underground mine, one that will tunnel beneath the wilderness from a mile outside its boundary. Soon the Cabinets may test whether modern mining and wilderness can coexist.

Chapter 4

Bob Marshall, Great Bear, Scapegoat

An expansive area where outfitters and guides keep America's wilderness dream alive

Hᴵɢʜ ᴀʟᴏɴɢ ᴛʜᴇ Cᴏɴᴛɪɴᴇɴᴛᴀʟ Dɪᴠɪᴅᴇ, the Chinese Wall rises like a wave of stone from a wilderness whose grandeur places it among the treasures of the American West. The limestone precipice towers 1,000 feet high and stretches north and south for a dozen miles. The shadowy cliffs form a soaring backdrop for an autumn pageant of rivalry as elk herds gather along the eastern foot of the wall, the bulls bugling and jousting for their harems in the alpine amphitheaters of the Sun River Game Preserve. High above, near the windswept tabletop of 8,539-foot Sphinx Peak, tawny ledges reveal stone impressions of seashells, suspended in time for 300 million years half a continent away from the sea.

To the west, far below in the South Fork valley of the Flathead River, trails wander for days along grassy river flats and wide gravel benches amid great ponderosa pines and Douglas firs that were already old when the pilgrims landed. To wander such a country—through the tall timber thickets, broad meadows, savannah, and silver-gray sage—is to glimpse a vestige of the great western Montana valleys that Meriwether Lewis and William Clark saw when the nation was still new.

This is the great Bob Marshall Wilderness, more than 1.5 million acres of wild land, a province larger than the state of Delaware. It is probably America's best-known wilderness, one that has been opened to thousands of visitors by a cadre of professional outfitters and guides who have led expeditions into its recesses for more than six decades. It is a land of goats, moose, lynx, and bighorn sheep, a place where golden eagles sail up out of deep timbered canyons on thermal currents, sweeping unexpectedly through ridge-top passes with the wind singing in their wings. It is a major ecosystem whose diversity ranges from

Big Salmon Lake reflects the diversity of America's best-known wilderness. The Bob Marshall country ranges from densely timbered valleys to snow-covered peaks. Holland Peak, center, is the 9,356-foot monarch of the Swan Range on the area's western edge.

glaciers and barren rocky pinnacles to broad timbered valleys and basin meadows where homesteaders once struggled for subsistence.

Together with Glacier National Park, it is the last stronghold in the lower 48 states for *Ursus arctos horribilis*, the mighty grizzly bear, the continent's most powerful beast and yet a threatened creature so secretive that even veteran wilderness travelers are lucky to glimpse one. It is a land of contrasts and changing moods. For every week of golden alpine sunshine, there is a week of slate sky and chilling rain, when all the world seems morose and senseless visions of the great bear may trouble your dreams. For some people this is a sacred land, a place of power that awakens and humbles the human spirit. It is a land still alive, still growing and changing as the forces of time, weather, and continental uplift mold and sculpt their work.

Today it is three wilderness areas in one, end-to-end, for 100 miles down the Continental Divide. Bounded by the Scapegoat Wilderness to the south and the Great Bear Wilderness to the north, the Bob Marshall is the centerpiece of a wilderness system that encompasses 2,398 square miles. It lends its name to the entire region, which is known to the managers and scientists as the Bob Marshall complex but to the outfitters as the Bob Marshall country, or simply the Bob.

The name honors a pioneering forester, conservationist, and patriarch of the American wilderness movement whose expeditions and writings earned him national renown in his own time. Marshall's vision helped awaken the U.S. Forest Service to the urgent need for preserving a portion of the vanishing wilderness from which the American heritage had been forged. Before his sudden illness and death in 1939, at age 38, he had secured the first protection for nearly 5.5 million acres, including the bulk of the area that was later to bear his name.

Bob Marshall sparked the wilderness dream, but the flame was kindled by the professional outfitters and guides who taught the secrets

of the wilderness to their countrymen. Extolled by those who came to know it and popularized in sporting and outdoor magazines, the Bob grew famous for its mountain grandeur, trophy big game, and fighting trout.

Today the outfitter industry is a $30 million-a-year bulwark of Montana's tourist economy, and the Bob Marshall complex accounts for perhaps $4 million of the total. Yet the industry groans under major stresses. In 2 decades, total use of the Bob has grown at twice the rate of the outfitter industry. Forest Service regulations governing outfitters have tightened, driving up costs. Fewer trips are permitted, fewer guests are allowed per trip, and outfitter fees are increasing sharply. Meanwhile, other visitors pay no use fees at all, and they enjoy total freedom from regulation. Their impacts are taking a toll on the pristine beauty of the Bob. Most outfitters support high standards for their industry, but a few complain of federal inflexibility and arbitrary interpretation of rules.

About 3,000 visitors a year ride the mountain trails of the Bob or float its wild rivers with outfitters to experience the land and discover its secrets. Shaped by long, north-south mountain ranges and river valleys, the wilderness holds a myriad of wonders: the Flathead Alps, a graceful

Meadows beneath the spectacular cliffs of the Chinese Wall, within the Sun River Game Preserve, left, are a gathering place for elk during their fall mating season. A 1,000-foot-high reef along 12 miles of the Continental Divide, the wall is one of the state's most prominent geologic features. So many wilderness visitors flock to the wall each year that special camping restrictions are necessary to protect the land. Relatively few people find their way to the equally magnificent cliffs north of Larch Hill Pass near Silvertip Mountain, far left on the horizon.

Dressing for the season, white-tailed ptarmigan, above, replace their brown summer plumage with white in winter. Moose, below, and black bears, facing page, live throughout the three-wilderness complex.

range of low alpine peaks adorned with high forests and meadows; Big Salmon Lake, 4 miles long and unspoiled by cabins or summer homes; and Needle Falls, where the White River drops into fractured limestone and then boils out of a needle-eyed orifice.

The western wilderness boundary follows the crest of the Swan Range, a rugged mountain front studded by more than a dozen small glaciers and dominated by the summits of 9,356-foot Holland Peak and 9,255-foot Swan Peak. The Continental Divide is the great central rib with the Chinese Wall at its midpoint. Nearly 30 miles south down the Divide, the huge massif of Scapegoat Mountain dominates the wilderness that shares its name. Guarded by cliff walls 1,500 feet high, Scapegoat's graceful 9,204-foot summit crowns a plateau 3 miles long. At the northern end of the complex, the Flathead Range angles northwest away from the Divide toward 8,705-foot Great Northern Mountain and Glacier National Park, its ridges shaping the northern panhandle of the Great Bear Wilderness.

The northern trident formed by the Swan, Flathead, and Continental Divide ranges is drained by two wild rivers: the South and Middle forks of the Flathead. Together with the North Fork adjoining Glacier Park, they form the nation's longest wild and scenic river system. The wilderness rivers are breeding grounds for the westslope blackspotted cutthroat trout, a genetic relic of the last Ice Age that has evolved to survive in the cold, pure waters of the western Montana Rockies. Scapegoat Mountain is the headwaters for the Dearborn River and for the North and Landers forks of the Blackfoot River. East of the Chinese Wall, the limestone cliffs roll out toward the plains like breakers toward a beach, forming the watershed for the North and South forks of the Sun River. At 9,392 feet, Rocky Mountain, the Bob's highest summit, dominates the western boundary.

More than 100 lakes dapple the high country, many of them clustered along the Swan Range or scattered across the southern end of the Scapegoat. Cutthroat trout predominate in lakes and rivers, but rainbow have been introduced in a few lakes, as have brown trout in parts of the Scapegoat. Huge Dolly Varden trout migrate up the Flathead to spawn in wilderness tributaries each fall.

Big game abounds. East of the Chinese Wall, an estimated 2,500 elk roam the sprawling 199,661-acre Sun River Game Preserve. The eastern edge of the preserve supports as many as 1,000 bighorn sheep. An estimated 255 to 335 grizzly bears wander the Bob Marshall ecosystem,

Winter is a season of extremes, when the Swan Range, above, changes into a land of sub-zero temperatures and howling blizzards. Hardy adventurers, facing page, find walking easier than skiing on the windswept rocks at Lion Creek Pass.

green mudstones from the west slid up and over the younger limestones, churning the earth's crust into chaotic blocks and slabs, pushing them ahead into great jumbled cliffs and walls. It was a collision in glacial slow motion, a few feet a century, one that might still be going on. Where the older mudstones rode up and over the younger limestones, an "overthrust" zone tens of miles wide resulted. Oil and gas seeps in the Bob entice petroleum geologists with the possibility that the younger, buried seabed rocks could yield oil and gas.

In such vast country it takes days to reach the heart of the wilderness and weeks to search out its soul. From early times, the Bob was horse country because trips required provisions that only pack trains could carry. Yet for all its mountains and distances, it was seldom formidable in summer and fall.

Early foresters built a network of fire trails soon after 1900, when solitary wilderness rangers patrolled ridge tops and watched for fires from lookout platforms built in trees. Today, the South Fork, Middle Fork, and Sun river valleys are major travel corridors, while pack trails wend high along the reef walls or up onto long ridges of grass and alpine timber. The valleys contain few obstacles other than streams, although these can be formidable to cross when swollen by snowmelt in May and June. Few are spanned by bridges. Trails over the major passes can be grueling, but mudholes and poor trail conditions are often more troublesome for hikers than the steep terrain.

About 60 outfitters lead guests into the three wilderness areas. Known for their rugged independence, outfitters are a remarkable breed of small businessmen who spend summers and falls shuttling supply trains over mountain heights, shepherding guests who may never have ridden a horse, and spinning tales around the camp stove at night. An outfitter and his wranglers often ride 2,000 miles in a single season. A 10-day hunt may cost $1,500 to $2,500 or more for dangerous quarry such as a grizzly. A summer horse or raft trip may run $50 to $100 a day. Some outfitters offer "drop camp" service. For $300 to $1,000, they will pack a hunter and his gear to a likely spot, drop him off for up to 10 days, and then pack him and his game out of the wilderness.

Hunting was the springboard for the outfitter industry as the lure of trophies brought big-game hunters, many of them wealthy executives, politicians, or celebrities. Some came as much for solitude and escape as for hunting. But the clientele has grown to include a diversity of small businessmen, factory workers, farmers, and retirees, some of whom may

the only place in the lower 48 states where grizzly hunting is still allowed. Up to 25 grizzlies may be killed each year, although the quota is rarely reached. Supporters argue that limited hunting culls grizzlies that are less wary of humans and more likely to pose a threat to them. Critics advocate a moratorium as long as the bear is threatened on its other ranges. The Bob has contributed to pioneering grizzly research by Dr. John Craighead, who has used Landsat earth satellite images to identify and map prime grizzly habitat. Even the movements of radio-collared animals can now be tracked by earth satellite.

The Bob lies just east of the Rocky Mountain trench, a zone where some geologists believe two ancient land masses collided a billion years ago. The rocks tell of a prehistoric sea that gradually filled with sediments eroded from ancient continents as life dawned and evolved into shelled mollusks. Perhaps 60 million years ago, at the end of the dinosaur era, the land west of the Bob was uplifted. Ancient purple and

save up for years for the experience. The outfitters cherish the land and are often in the vanguard of movements to expand the wilderness system. They view their way of life as the passport that opens the wilderness to many Americans who would otherwise never experience it.

"I've met a lot of wonderful people from all walks of life, from those who had to save 2 or 3 years to those who could really afford it," says Art Weikum, who has packed into the White River since 1952. Some find the wilderness overwhelming. "Just the size of it—they can't comprehend it." A Pennsylvania congressman once told Weikum he wanted to leave after only 2 days. "He said, 'I've got to get out. The vastness is closing in on me,' " Weikum recalls. "I know what he meant. It's the same feeling I've had a few times in town."

Even in such vastness, outfitters are competing for elbow room. Today they are far outnumbered by private parties. The growth in use has brought changes, impacts, and conflicts typified by the decade-long controversy over "caches."

Early outfitter camps were often luxurious to excess, with visitors treated to private tent cabins, beds, carpeted floors, bathing or shower facilities, and sumptuous meals complete with china and wine glasses.

Like flames in the forest, virgin stands of Western larch fill the wilderness with autumn color. Unlike most conifers, larch drop their needles in fall. Danaher Creek, facing page, meanders through broad meadows near the headwaters of the Flathead River's South Fork. Lush river bottoms are important spring habitat for one of the last stable populations of grizzly bears in the lower 48 states. The valleys make convenient travel corridors through the wilderness, but even on horseback it can take days to reach the area's interior.

Even today, the lavish food served up to weary hunters or riders is a hallmark of wilderness travel. Opulence was in keeping with an age when grand hotels were rising in the national parks and the prevailing philosophy held that visitors should be able to discover their wild heritage in absolute comfort. But it led to the use of caches—small structures where heavy stoves or other equipment could be stored. Log tent frames were left in place year-round, as were corrals, outhouses, and hitching rails. Some camps took on the appearance of permanent settlements deep in a land that was supposed to be untouched by human development. As criticism mounted and the Forest Service pressed for cleanup, outfitters split over the use of caches. Some relinquished them willingly. Others argued that they were insignificant compared to the network of Forest Service cabins, ranger stations, and phone lines still in place from the pre-wilderness period. Caches reduced the number of pack train trips required to haul equipment over trails that the Forest Service was already hard-pressed to maintain. Some saw the elimination of caches as Forest Service retaliation for outfitter support of wilderness laws that in effect took away Forest Service management prerogatives and ordered the agency to protect wilderness. "They were going to ram it down our throats," one outfitter says.

Today, caches are largely gone. Tent frames are taken down when not in use. Sacrifices in comfort have been minimal. Camps are smaller and more congenial. Modern technology has replaced the bulky trappings of luxury with comparable equipment that is lighter and more efficient.

Outfitter Arnold "Smoke" Elser, who has spent 25 seasons in the Scapegoat, has earned a reputation as a leader in developing better methods. His camp is compact. His single hunting tent is divided into three sections: guests bunk at one end and hired hands at the other, and the kitchen occupies the middle. His entire summer kitchen folds into a compact box. Portable corrals hold stock. A collapsible kitchen stove he designed contains a water jacket to heat water more efficiently.

An advocate of no-trace camping, Elser tells his guests about a friendly game he plays with outfitter Jack Hooker. They pretend they are outlaws fleeing from the sheriff. Though each knows where the other is going, each tries to keep the other from discovering exactly where he has been. That means all litter is scrupulously picked up, horse manure is kicked around and scattered, woodcutting is forbidden in camp, and the sod is removed before any campfires and carefully replanted afterward.

Braided channels of the South Fork of the Flathead carve through the heart of the Bob. River guides lead trips through the Flathead's challenging Middle Fork, facing page. Along with the North Fork, the rivers form the nation's longest wild and scenic river system.

If one finds evidence of the other's passing, the other gets a razzing at their next encounter. Elser believes wilderness impacts would all but disappear if everyone shared his outlaw fantasy.

Intent on reducing impacts, Forest Service managers have steadily tightened the reins on outfitters. Party sizes have been reduced. Where 35 guests were once common, now 10 is a large party and 15 is maximum. Total trips per outfitter have been limited. Fees are slated to increase from 25 cents a visitor-day to 3 percent of the guest's gross fee. Outfitters are required to file itineraries months in advance and to pack in hay and feed for livestock. Camps are under close scrutiny, each regulated under a camp operating plan approved by the Forest Service. No new outfitter permits are being issued. Though most outfitters maintain high standards, occasionally one will cause a glaring problem. An outfitter camp abandoned in the Great Bear in late 1982 was a startling eyesore the next spring. Outfitters face loss of their permits for failure to clean up camps and meet deadlines. Yet some complain of arbitrary decisions that seem needlessly harsh. One outfitter's permit was revoked because he was 4

days late meeting a deadline for camp changes that he had appealed. An appeal can take months in the federal bureaucracy, and court action is not allowed until the federal appeal process is completed. Most outfitters believe high standards are essential to protect the wilderness, but many feel they have been singled out by a Forest Service that is politically nervous about attacking the real problem: the backcountry impacts of an unregulated public.

Travel statistics show the visitor trends. In 1960, only about 3,500 persons visited the Bob Marshall. Half came in summer and half during the hunting season. One-third traveled with outfitters. Fewer than 5 percent were backpackers. By 1981, an estimated 8,000 visitors and 12,000 horses and pack animals entered the Bob on only 8 of its major trails. Total visitors were probably at least double that number. Only 17 percent traveled with outfitters. More than one-third of the visitors were hikers. A startling 73 percent of all visitors were not affiliated with any organized conservation or user group.

Simply gathering statistics on wilderness use is difficult. Only one visitor in five bothers to fill out a voluntary trip registration card provided at wilderness entry portals. To get better visitor counts, wilderness management expert Bob Lucas of the Missoula Forestry Sciences Laboratory set up automatic cameras near major entrance points.

With unaffiliated users now in the vast majority, rangers are hard-pressed to contact visitors and teach the new ethic of no-trace camping. Traditional meetings with organized outfitters, sportsmen, horsemen, and wilderness groups no longer include most users. Meanwhile, the marks of overuse and carelessness increase along popular routes. Heavier use also means more wear and tear on trails, especially in wet seasons. Trails in wet areas degenerate into mudholes and grow ever wider as travelers detour around them, especially where trails were built on terrain unsuitable for heavy use. Money for relocating them is scarce. A wet summer such as 1983 aggravates the problem.

"We spent an extra $10,000 on the Holland Trail" in 1983, says retired wilderness ranger Cal Tassinari, "but I defy you to show me where that money was spent." He says many trails cannot take the punishment of heavy horse traffic coupled with wet weather. Increasing use in early spring compounds the damage.

"I go along with this ecology thing," says outfitter Jack Hooker, who has packed into the Bob for 30 years. "You get very religious about this

The highest peaks contain reminders of the time, eons ago, when the northern Rocky Mountains formed the bed of a prehistoric sea. Fossilized shellfish, left, are one of many ancient species found petrified in rock above 8,000 feet near Trilobite Peak. The old seabed was uplifted by geologic forces and later carved by glaciers to form today's rugged mountains and valleys, facing page. In the Great Bear Wilderness, the scalloped surface of melting snow overlooks Dolly Varden Creek, with the peaks of Glacier National Park on the horizon.

country after you've operated in here so many years. It really hurts me to see private parties set up here and leave a big goddamn mess. I clean up after all these guys. You can't help but be a little jealous about this country."

Hooker guides hunters along the southwestern boundary between the Bob and Scapegoat from a camp in the Danaher Basin where Danaher Creek, a tributary of the South Fork, meanders across a luxuriant mountain meadow. But he is worried about the growth in visitor pressure. "Now we're seeing hordes of private parties," he says. In 1983, the first week of hunting season found 11 hunting camps set up along the Danaher. Hooker says he does not mind private parties, but they should be limited, to protect the hunting quality for everyone.

"I don't think it's fair to over-regulate outfitters when you're not regulating anybody else," adds outfitter Ron Curtiss. He believes restrictive rules directed at outfitters discriminate indirectly against their clients, citizens who live far away from the wilderness and are least able to enjoy it on their own.

"They should stop looking at this as outfitters versus the public," he argues. "This is the outfitted public versus the non-outfitted public."

A glaring example of careless outfitting practices, such as the pile of trash at a hunting camp near Scott Lake in the Great Bear, right, can focus greater public attention on professional wilderness guides and trigger stricter regulation of their back-country operations. Most outfitters have a deep love for and understanding of the land, which they treat with respect. The rising popularity of wilderness recreation is forcing professionals and amateurs alike to adopt new, no-trace camping techniques to protect the area's pristine quality.

Illegal "rogue" outfitters also compete with licensed ones, bringing in guests who are passed off as personal friends. Rogue operations are tough to crack, according to Bill Maloit, state supervisor of outfitting, who has patrolled the Bob for 36 years. Undercover agents pose as clients to expose such operations. The state won 18 convictions in 1983 alone. Still, Maloit says the typical fine is $300, "a very minimal business expense," and the rogue becomes more wary after he is caught.

Administrative changes that create new wilderness attractions also bring additional users. Deep in the Great Bear at the Schafer Ranger Station, a grass airstrip offers the only public air access to the wilderness for commercial pilots, outfitters, river-runners, or private parties who feel like dropping in for an afternoon wilderness picnic. The rasping drone of aircraft fills the Middle Fork canyon at regular intervals as light planes burst over the crest of the Flathead Range and shuttle in with their cargoes of rafts, supplies, and visitors. Other airstrips provide access just outside the wilderness at Benchmark and Spotted Bear. The thrill of soaring high over the wilderness can be an annoyance to those far below trying to escape civilization.

The Schafer airstrip was a fixture long before Congress officially

34

Pancakes in paradise are among the luxuries outfitters provide their guests. A leader in backcountry innovations, Smoke Elser, left, packs in all the comforts of home without any of the mess. Elser's camp, with a lightweight folding stove and specially designed tents, is a model of orderliness. In addition to protecting wilderness resources, clean, simple camps allow more time to enjoy the area. Wranglers, below, find time for an evening shave near Meadow Creek, while guests relax after a trail ride in the Scapegoat Wilderness.

35

designated the Great Bear Wilderness in 1978. It jumped in popularity after 1976, when the Middle Fork officially became a wild river. The law creating the Great Bear specifically allowed the airstrip to remain open, a provision that did little to quell opposition to wilderness from organized pilots. The law also stipulated that air traffic at Schafer should remain at 1978 levels. That provision leaves managers in a no-win situation. Soon they will be forced to limit air traffic and face the wrath of those who get turned away.

Confronted by these and other problems, foresters are rethinking traditional approaches to wilderness management. The challenge is to develop innovative ways to manage the people who visit the Bob without tampering with the wilderness or inhibiting the wilderness experience. Rejecting the idea of permit systems, with their arbitrary quotas, burdensome reservations, and travel schedules, managers have decided instead to develop methods for measuring the subtle changes that add up to impacts. They hope to define the "limits of acceptable change"—the thresholds at which problems become public nuisances that interfere with the wilderness experience. Led by Jerry Stokes of the Flathead National Forest, a task force representing a broad cross section of wilderness users has spent more than two years defining limits and ways to measure them. If it works, the new approach may make it easier to educate wilderness users about impacts and to decide when field rangers should temporarily close specific sites and ask visitors to give them a rest.

Most problem visitors are not aware that they are causing damage, says Gordon Ash, seasonal ranger at the old Big Prairie wilderness ranger station—now a work center for trail crews. Ash prefers to explain low-impact techniques rather than write tickets.

Some wilderness trends affect outfitters in subtle ways. Decades of forest fire control have resulted in a loss of elk range, new forests having taken over old burns. Between 1889 and 1934, more than one-third of the Bob burned in major fires that created transitional elk ranges of brush and undergrowth while new trees were sprouting. Elk herds thrived, helping to build the Bob's reputation as a big-game paradise. By the early 1930s, they had outstripped their relatively small wintering areas along the valley bottoms. Massive winter kills followed, with as many as 500 dead elk counted in a single 10-mile stretch along the South Fork after the hard winter of 1933.

"When I first came into this country, there was more elk than I ever saw before," Hooker says. Numbers declined greatly by the late 1950s,

Clusters of yellow comb draba blossoms, above, adorn the Scapegoat in early summer. The North Fork of the Blackfoot River, facing page, rages through a narrow canyon. Once chosen as a potential hydroelectric dam site, the river's power remains unbridled.

but he believes the elk are increasing again. To help restore the natural cycle of wilderness fire, managers have developed fire plans based on research from the Selway-Bitterroot Wilderness. If fires start naturally under favorable conditions in areas that could benefit from fire, they will be allowed to burn.

Outfitters and conservationists, once at odds over wilderness purity, have become allies recently in an effort to protect the wilderness. Both have helped build a national constituency to defend the Bob against outside exploitation. The first major battle was waged 30 years ago over Forest Service plans to develop roads through what is now the Great Bear. "We had 6,000 names on petitions against that," says 70-year-old Dallas Eklund of Kalispell, recalling the "Battle of Bunker Creek."

Until a decade ago, early planning was underway for a major dam at Spruce Park, on the Middle Fork. The plan included a reservoir in what is now the Great Bear, with a tunnel beneath the Flathead Range to divert water to Hungry Horse Reservoir. In 1976, the dam proposal died when the Middle Fork won protection as a wild river.

Outfitters and wilderness groups joined forces to seek preservation for the Scapegoat Wilderness when roads and timber sales were mapped out in the late 1960s. The decision to fight for a wilderness was made at the ranch of the late outfitter "Hobnail" Tom Edwards. A major trail into the Scapegoat today bears Edwards' name.

Even after an area becomes wilderness, outfitters and others often must continue the fight to guard it from change. One plan advanced a decade ago would have caused watershed changes that some believed would harm wildlife and shorten visitor seasons. Water from the wilderness passes through 16 dams en route down the Columbia River to the sea. During a 1973 drought, the Bonneville Power Administration proposed cloudseeding to increase the wilderness snowpack and augment the regional water supply. At the time, the agency estimated that a 10 percent increase in the Bob's snowpack would yield electricity for 15,000 homes. The plan died when the drought suddenly ended.

The most recent confrontation was a classic environmental battle over the threatened "bombing of the Bob." The promise of oil and gas from the overthrust touched off a wave of exploration and speculation in the late 1970s, culminating in a 1980 request by a Denver firm to plant explosive charges along 207 miles of seismic lines crisscrossing the wilderness. The idea was to generate underground shock waves that could be plotted electronically to locate possible oil and gas reserves. The request triggered a storm of protest, resulting in thousands of letters and a march on the regional forester's office in Missoula. Opponents cited estimates indicating that at best the wilderness would yield only enough energy to fuel the nation's needs for a few days. To marshal opposition, some outfitters alerted former clients through newsletters, while others contacted former guests in high corporate and government places who could carry messages of concern directly to the administration and Congress. In the end, Regional Forester Tom Coston, backed by Forest Service Chief Max Peterson, rejected the application.

With both a far-reaching constituency and an economic importance to Montana, the Bob is one of the most secure American wilderness areas. Yet its recent history shows that it is not immune to outside pressures. The American experiment in wilderness preservation, unprecedented in human history and scarcely one generation old, may not survive the test of time and the ambitions of men. If it does, a large part of the credit will go to the hardy breed of modern mountain men who have staked their careers on it in order to bring it to life for others.

37

Chapter 5

RED ROCK LAKES, UL BEND, MEDICINE LAKE

Small remnants of wilderness providing refuge for America's wildest creatures

UPPER RED ROCK LAKE comes alive as the first golden streaks of dawn ease over the Continental Divide. A lesser scaup noisily announces the morning, accompanied by mallards quacking along the shore. Sandhill cranes cry shrilly as they pace the rolling grassland overlooking the lake. Nearby, pronghorn antelope sprint across the sagebrush-covered floor of the mountain valley. From one of the lake's secluded bays, two trumpeter swans add their deep, resonant bugling to the growing cacophony. The great swans unfurl their broad wings and spring into the morning air, winging high over Montana's Red Rock Lakes Wilderness.

The swans rise over a land of lakes, marshes, and high prairies hemmed by the towering Centennial Mountains and the gentle foothills of the Gravelly Range. Red Rock is one of the last strongholds of the trumpeter swan, among the rarest and most majestic birds on the continent. Once pushed to the brink of extinction, the swans, like many of America's wildest creatures, have found a haven in the wilderness.

Montana has three wildlife wildernesses: Red Rock Lakes, UL Bend, and Medicine Lake. The diverse areas are part of the national wildlife refuge system and are managed by the U.S. Fish and Wildlife Service more for the benefit of birds and animals than for the pleasure of people. In a world where man's activities have changed much of the natural environment, wilderness areas like these contain the undisturbed habitat that many species of wildlife need to survive.

Nestled in Beaverhead County's strikingly beautiful Centennial Valley, about 50 miles west of Yellowstone National Park, Red Rock is a 32,000-acre wilderness within a 40,000-acre national wildlife refuge. Nearly all the wilderness is covered by water. The large, shallow Upper

The calm water of Upper Red Rock Lake reflects a dazzling sunrise over mountains and marshes. A land of solitude, where man is but an occasional visitor, Red Rock offers sanctuary to a diverse community of wildlife, including the rare trumpeter swan.

and Lower Red Rock lakes are the heart of an extensive system of marshes tied together by meandering Red Rock Creek. From the 6,600-foot valley floor, the wilderness rises to the crest of the 10,000-foot-high Centennials, a rare east-to-west mountain range.

Red Rock is a drive-in wilderness. A gravel road skirts its edge, where campgrounds, complete with picnic tables and barbecue pits, overlook the marsh. Despite the relatively easy access, this is one of the least visited wilderness areas in Montana. Few of the 6,000 people who find their way into this isolated valley each year venture beyond the edge of the wilderness. Although game and cattle trails wander through the dryland portions of the area, the short boat ramps leading onto Upper and Lower Red Rock lakes are the only semblance of developed trails. The proposed Continental Divide Trail would parallel the southern boundary of the area, but the best means of exploring Red Rock's wilderness interior is by canoe. Boats are allowed on Upper Red Rock Lake only after July 15, when the waterfowl nesting season ends. Motorboats are permitted on Lower Red Rock Lake in the fall, a concession Congress made to the duck hunters who had boated on the lake for decades before it became a wilderness. Boating is prohibited on the lower lake during the spring and summer to protect nesting swans.

For about 5 months each year, the valley is virtually locked away from the rest of the world by 3 to 16 feet of snow. The few people who live in Lakeview, a rustic resort town and Fish and Wildlife Service outpost on the southern fringe of the refuge, are a 30-mile snowmobile ride from civilization during the long winter.

Red Rock's unusual melding of native grassland, marshes, and mountains creates habitat for a diverse community of wildlife. Moose roam the Centennials and adjoining Henrys Lake Mountains. The moose population increases greatly in the fall as animals from surrounding mountains drop into the wilderness to winter in the willow

39

On a mission of mercy, biologist Terry McEneaney, above, maneuvers into place a floating platform designed to protect nests and precious swan eggs from flood waters.

thickets on the valley floor. The dryland areas bordering the marsh are home to 300 to 500 pronghorns, a large herd for the relatively compact area. Mule deer, elk, and black bears inhabit the forests, joined by an occasional grizzly drifting in from Yellowstone Park or the nearby Targhee National Forest of Idaho.

Most visitors come to fish Red Rock Creek or several small lakes that are in the refuge, but outside the wilderness. The creek holds one of Montana's last populations of native arctic grayling. Grayling thrived throughout the upper Missouri River and its tributaries until pollution and sedimentation in streams and rivers forced the sail-winged fish to retreat, like the trumpeter swan, into pockets of still-suitable habitat. Nearby, Elk, Culver, and MacDonald lakes boast trophy-sized rainbow, eastern brook, and Yellowstone cutthroat trout. The wilderness lakes and ponds, inhabited mostly by small ling and suckers, are closed to fishing to protect wildlife from disturbance by humans.

Red Rock is perhaps most remarkable for its bird life. Bald and golden eagles, sora rails, peregrine falcons, and 23 kinds of ducks and geese are among the 215 species of birds found in the wilderness. The marshes offer a resting spot for tens of thousands of migrating waterfowl each year, while providing enough nesting habitat to produce as many as 8,000 ducks each summer. But it is as a sanctuary for trumpeter swans, the largest birds in North America, that Red Rock is best known.

This area was preserved for the sake of the trumpeters, which are bigger, deeper-voiced cousins of the more common tundra or whistling swans. The great birds were once so numerous throughout the country that their snowy plumage was used to make powder puffs and writing quills. But market hunters killed them by the thousands, and an expanding nation of settlers drained their marshes and destroyed their habitat. In 1935, with the 70 known remaining swans surviving within a short radius of the Centennial Valley, the federal government created Red Rock Lakes National Wildlife Refuge. And in 1976, Congress added another layer of regulatory protection to the irreplaceable marsh by naming it a wilderness area.

Abandoned homesteads weathering on the edge of the wilderness are testament to the hard life settlers found when they arrived here a century ago. This valley is no more hospitable to the trumpeter swan than it was to the homesteader. Red Rock provides only marginal habitat. The winters are long and severe, and the short summers allow only one chance a year for nesting. Yet the area offers the wary, easily disturbed birds what they need most: safety and security. The swan population rebounded dramatically on the wilderness preserve. The regional trumpeter population in Red Rock, Yellowstone Park, and the Henrys Fork of the Snake River peaked at about 670 birds in 1958.

But the regional swan population and production of young, called cygnets, have declined markedly in recent years, a trend biologists cannot fully explain. Poor weather for nesting accounts for part of the decline. Although a nesting pair of swans hatches two to seven cygnets every summer, only a fraction survive. About one-half the region's cygnets are raised in Red Rock, with about 30 surviving to flight each year. However, healthy populations of trumpeters have been discovered in Alaska and Canada, and fear for the bird's extinction has eased.

A regal trio wings gracefully past the Centennial Mountains. Two swans wear collars that help managers identify the birds. Nesting pairs, above left, remain mates for life.

41

Most of the swans spend their lives near Red Rock, no longer migrating to warmer winter climes. More than 250 swans winter on Culver and MacDonald lakes on the eastern end of the refuge. Unlike the vast wilderness marsh, the two small lakes are spring-fed and do not freeze. However, the area lacks enough natural food to sustain the swans through the winter, so the Fish and Wildlife Service feeds them grain.

Red Rock's wilderness designation protects it from mining and petroleum exploration. Wilderness restrictions also guard the timbered slopes against logging. Although government grazing allotments allow cattle to feed side by side with pronghorns, ranchers are prohibited from using motor vehicles to tend their herds. All these protections help preserve the tranquility so important to the stately trumpeters. Yet for the swans, and for many other types of wildlife that live in wilderness areas, strict regulations can hurt as well as help.

Although Congress gave the Fish and Wildlife Service permission to use a motorboat for capturing and banding swans, wildlife in wilderness must be managed without leaving man's imprint on nature. For example, the many miles of fences that separate cattle from swan habitat must be maintained without the aid of vehicles or power tools. Without the help of modern equipment, prescribed burning to improve

Pronghorn antelope are common on Red Rock's rolling grasslands. Tolerant of man's disruptions, pronghorns prosper in much of Montana.

habitat is difficult, at best. Even the winter feeding, which may be essential to the swans' survival, seems to clash with the spirit of the Wilderness Act. However, an attempt to restore natural conditions by forcing the birds to seek more suitable wintering grounds failed: when the winter grain supplements were withheld, about 30 swans died before refuge managers abandoned the experiment and resumed the feeding.

Some biologists have suggested that rescinding Red Rock's wilderness designation might allow better, more intensive wildlife management. But, aware that the unprecedented step would take an act of Congress and create a political firestorm, agency officials are not seriously pursuing the idea. Instead, wildlife managers at Red Rock are concentrating their efforts on understanding more about the swans and the wilderness where they live. One management project involves rebuilding swan nests atop floating platforms to protect eggs from flooding. The platforms promise to increase the swans' nesting success without requiring humans to alter significantly the wild environment.

Although there is hope for the trumpeter's survival, chances may be limited for restoring widespread populations of the birds in the continental United States. Biologists have succeeded in transplanting some swans in other areas where the birds once lived. But few of the

Red Rock is a wilderness for creatures great and small. Willow thickets provide good moose habitat; curiosity lures a fox kit from its den.

43

UL Bend, left, has changed little since the first steamboat stopped along its shores. Prairie dogs fill a vital niche in the prairie ecosystem.

relocated swans prosper. People have ruined too many of America's natural places, leaving little more than the marshy wilderness of Red Rock Lakes where the trumpeters can sing their wild song.

In the not-so-distant past, all Montana was a wilderness for wildlife, especially the broad, rolling plains east of the Rocky Mountains. Tremendous herds of bison roamed the prairie, along with elk, wild sheep, and grizzlies. But America's westward expansion destroyed much of the wilderness and its wild inhabitants. Market hunters all but wiped out the bison. The native prairie grasses, which had supported an amazing diversity of life for thousands of years, fell to the homesteader's plow. Settlers pushed the elk into the mountains and drove the Audubon sheep to extinction. The newcomers also killed or chased from the land the Indians who for so long had shared the prairie with the wildlife.

On their way West, uncounted numbers of settlers crossed an area known as UL Bend, a narrow peninsula along a sweeping hairpin turn in the Missouri River. Located in Phillips County, midway between Lewistown and Glasgow, UL Bend is now a 20,800-acre wilderness area. It lacks the spectacular landscape of Montana's mountain wildernesses but possesses a harsh beauty. Short prairie grasses wave in the incessant wind amid clusters of prickly pear cactus. Sagebrush and greasewood cover broad flats, where patches of snow-white alkali bake in the sun.

45

Although sometimes inhospitable, the short-grass prairie rolls out a welcome mat of blue penstemon and other wildflowers in spring.

Small forests of scrawny ponderosa pine and juniper fill a winding series of coulees.

The land in the wilderness interior rolls gently, but the serpentine edges of the area fall ruggedly to the shores of Fort Peck Lake, the impounded waters of the Missouri River. UL Bend lies a short distance downstream from the last free-flowing section of the 2,500-mile-long Missouri. The lake, a mile wide at its narrowest point, forms a broad moat protecting 32 miles of shoreline on the eastern, southern, and western boundaries of the wilderness. Thousands of acres of federal and state land adjoin the northern boundary. From the lakeshore at 2,250 feet above sea level, the land rises steeply. But the highest point in the area, near the southern end of the peninsula, reaches only 2,700 feet.

UL Bend is the legacy left by glaciers. During a series of ice ages, thick sheets of ice pushed the Missouri River out of its historic channel, which is now occupied by the Milk River, 60 miles to the north. The Missouri carved its present channel along the southern face of the glaciers, detouring in a great bend around the finger of ice that extended over what is now UL Bend. The glaciers covered large expanses of Bearpaw shale, an easily eroded type of decomposed bedrock. Water melting from the southern face of the glaciers flowed into the Missouri River, carving deep ravines as it tumbled across the Bearpaw shale. The ravines form today's Missouri River Breaks.

The Breaks and prairie appear barren at midday but change dramatically when late-afternoon shadows fill the swales and coulees. Evening brings the wildlife out of hiding to feed on grasses and shrubs. This narrow peninsula supports a surprisingly large population of mule deer, as well as white-tailed deer, pronghorns, and elk. A variety of birds and smaller animals, from burrowing owls to prairie dogs, inhabit the area. Yet the UL Bend is more than a wildlife refuge; this remarkable wilderness is a portal into Montana's past.

A thick layer of whitened bones at the base of a cutbank tells of a time, perhaps 500 years ago, when herds of American bison thundered across this plain. The bones undoubtedly mark a buffalo jump, where Indians killed bison by stampeding them over a steep embankment. The last bison vanished from this area more than a century ago, but their weathered horns still remain scattered across the sage flats. Large circles of rocks, undisturbed for centuries, mark the spots where Sioux, Blackfeet, and Crow tribes pitched their tepees when they came here to hunt.

The earth, especially along the lakeshore, contains evidence of life in a much earlier time. The ground holds a wide array of fossils, including wood, shellfish, and bones. Fossils, Indian artifacts, and other historic items are for the looking, not taking, however; Fish and Wildlife Service regulations prohibit collecting them.

The Lewis and Clark expedition found an area teeming with wildlife when it passed UL Bend in late May 1805. The party camped at the mouth of the Musselshell River, just across the Missouri River from the southern tip of UL Bend's peninsula. As the explorers approached UL Bend, the expedition's Sergeant John Ordway noted in his journal that "we saw large gangs of elk, which are getting more plenty than the buffalo." The journals of Lewis and Clark say the party also saw many Canada geese and killed several grizzlies near UL Bend.

Although the elk and geese were once driven from the plains, both were reintroduced in the 1950s, and small populations have been restored. The UL Bend and the surrounding Charles M. Russell National Wildlife Refuge are the only places in Montana where elk still occupy their native prairie year-round. Grizzlies, however, retreated to

Nature was reclaiming an old trail, right, when fishermen persuaded Congress to call the wheel ruts a road. Dead sage now defines one of the first roads opened in a wilderness.

The blazing sun slowly yields to night over UL Bend. Bold sunsets inspired artist Charles M. Russell, after whom a nearby refuge is named.

the mountains, never to return to their home on the plains.

People tried but failed to tame this piece of wild prairie. The steamboats that began plying the Missouri River in 1859 stopped at the UL Bend, which was known then as the Great Bend of the Missouri. The steamboats discharged passengers on the area's eastern shore, giving river-weary people a chance to stretch their legs with a 2-mile walk across the peninsula. The steamboats picked up the passengers again on the western shore after chugging around the bend. Today, a number of faint trails cross the peninsula at its narrowest point, perhaps the pathways left by some of the earliest Montanans.

Ranchers and homesteaders tried to settle here. The area's name comes from the UL brand borne by the cattle that once ranged over the peninsula. But the harsh climate and rough terrain of the Missouri River Breaks defeated those who tried to stake claim to the wilderness. "Man has never been very successful at doing anything in the Breaks that was able to overcome what Mother Nature wants to do here," says Jim McCollum of the Fish and Wildlife Service.

On the area's western ridge, grass almost covers a wooden hay rake, an artifact hauled up from the homesteads that were obliterated when Fort Peck Lake flooded the Missouri River bottoms in 1941. A cowboy's old line camp, consisting of a pair of aging log cabins, still stands on a

low hill overlooking Jim Wells Creek, near the northern end of the wilderness. Water, potable but soured by minerals, bubbles from an artesian well a short distance from the cabins. Two rusting wire fences, which the Fish and Wildlife Service hopes to remove someday, bisect the area.

Although the wilderness contains no maintained trails, several twin-rutted tracks wend through the area. Horse-drawn wagons probably laid down the first tracks, but four-wheel-drive vehicles etched them firmly in the soil. The area was open to vehicles until it became a wilderness area in 1976.

An occasional survey marker pokes above the low sage, miniature memorials to a grandiose scheme that would have turned the UL Bend into a nesting marsh for waterfowl. When the Fish and Wildlife Service established the UL Bend National Wildlife Refuge in 1967, its officials envisioned crisscrossing the flats with a series of low dikes, then flooding the area with water pumped from the Missouri River. Nine years later, with the project doomed by economic reality, the agency asked Congress to designate the area as wilderness.

Although UL Bend's wilderness designation came without much organized public support or opposition, the area later became the focus of a minor political skirmish in Congress. Led by Montana Sen. John Melcher, Congress in 1983 pried open a narrow corridor through one corner of the wilderness—an act that allows vehicles to travel one of the old jeep trails through the UL Bend to reach Fort Peck Lake.

Regardless of the road, the Fish and Wildlife Service figures that only about 4,000 people visit the UL Bend each year. Ease of access to UL Bend is fair to terrible, depending on the weather. In warm, dry weather, the wilderness is a 50-mile dirt-road drive from the town of Zortman, near Highway 191. After a heavy rain, the entire expanse surrounding UL Bend becomes a wilderness of gumbo, impassable even for four-wheel-drive vehicles.

UL Bend is at its best in late spring, when the prairie blooms with penstemon and yellow pea. Spring temperatures are balmy compared to the often-searing heat of summer and the sometimes-frigid cold of winter. But most wilderness visitors arrive during the fall, attracted by big game and upland-game-bird hunting seasons. The number of backpackers who explore UL Bend in a given year is minuscule.

For early settlers, UL Bend was a small obstacle on a long westward journey. Similarly, most of today's Montanans and the tourists who visit

Graceful in flight, awkward at landing, white pelicans join a nesting colony on Big Island in Medicine Lake, Montana's smallest wilderness.

the state pass the area by, choosing instead to search for outdoor adventures in some of the better-known mountain wildernesses. The rolling peninsula remains a quiet refuge for wildlife and an almost-forgotten reminder of Montana's pristine past.

At another wildland remnant, Medicine Lake Wilderness, people are looking to the future. In the middle of a region dominated by intensive agriculture, the Fish and Wildlife Service is working to ensure the survival of a small enclave of northeastern Montana's prairie.

The state's smallest wilderness, Medicine Lake is a sample of the marsh-filled prairie that once stretched across northeastern Montana into Canada, the Dakotas, and Minnesota. After a century of farming and development, most of the wild prairies around Medicine Lake have been plowed and the marshes drained to make room for farms.

The 11,800-acre wilderness is within Medicine Lake National Wildlife Refuge in Sheridan and Roosevelt counties, located between Sidney and Plentywood. The wilderness consists of 8,700-acre Medicine Lake and the Sand Hills, a tiny relic of eastern Montana's mixed-grass prairie. Medicine Lake is a point of transition between the short-grass prairie of central Montana and the tall-grass prairie of the Great Plains.

Islands in the lake support one of the continent's largest remaining nesting colonies of white pelicans, big, graceful birds whose numbers

49

have been depleted through pesticide poisoning and lost habitat. About 3,500 pelicans return to Medicine Lake each spring. The wilderness lake also offers occasional refuge to the perilously endangered whooping cranes, which pass by on their migration between their northern Canada nesting area and their wintering grounds on the Gulf of Mexico.

Great blue herons, double-crested cormorants, and two species of gulls also nest here, along with most species of North American ducks. Nesting waterfowl produce more than 25,000 ducks and nearly 1,000 Canada geese annually. Between 100,000 and 250,000 waterfowl sojourn at Medicine Lake during spring and fall migrations.

The lake portion of the wilderness offers migratory birds a much-needed sanctuary. On a continent where wetlands are disappearing rapidly in the name of human progress, Medicine Lake and its islands offer birds and other wildlife a secure place to rest or nest. Perhaps the greatest danger to bird life here is the naturally occurring outbreaks of botulism. The periodic disease kills ducks by the thousands, forcing wildlife managers to invade the wilderness lake with motorboats to pick up carcasses in hopes of controlling its spread.

Where herds of bison once ranged, the grasslands surrounding Medicine Lake now support nearly 1,200 white-tailed deer. Pronghorns frequented the area less than a decade ago but have nearly vanished from the wilderness in recent years. Large numbers of sharp-tail grouse and ring-necked pheasants also live in the prairie portions.

Wildlife has almost always been plentiful here. Assiniboine Indians used to hunt bison near Medicine Lake. Today, the area's plentiful deer, waterfowl, and upland game bird populations still attract hunters. Fishermen seek Medicine Lake's northern pike. But many of the 9,000 people who visit here each year come simply to watch the birds and animals.

Medicine Lake occupies a portion of the Missouri River's ancestral bed. The glaciers that forced the river to change its course to the south more than 10,000 years ago also leveled the land. When the glaciers retreated, they left behind huge pieces of buried ice that melted to form Medicine Lake and other prairie potholes. Windblown sand from Medicine Lake's ancient shore later drifted into dunes, forming the foundation beneath today's Sand Hills.

Although farming altered much of the native prairie pothole country, farmers and their livestock are playing an important new role in the protection of the pure native grassland at Medicine Lake.

Government agencies allow livestock grazing in most wilderness areas. At Medicine Lake, wilderness managers use an intensive grazing program to help native prairie grasses compete against an invasion of crested wheatgrass, an exotic variety introduced by homesteaders. Gene Stroops, manager of Medicine Lake National Wildlife Refuge, worries that crested wheatgrass from surrounding lands will eventually spread

throughout the Sand Hills, effectively destroying the unique area.

The refuge is using cattle to combat the problem, allowing the animals to graze wheatgrass-infested areas early in the spring. Because wheatgrass greens up earlier than prairie grasses, the cattle eat it instead of the native varieties. Land managers move the cattle out of the area before the native species begin greening up, giving the plants a competitive edge against the wheatgrass.

Only time will reveal whether grazing is the ultimate defense for this parcel of native prairie. For now, the tactic seems to be working, and life for the birds and animals of Medicine Lake continues much as always. Nearby, traffic speeds by on state Highway 16. Farmers guide their tractors through surrounding fields, and oil rigs on distant ridges draw from the earth the lifeblood of energy-hungry America. But on spring mornings, sharp-tail grouse still gather near the lake, as they have for centuries, to perform their bizarre courtship dance. Pelicans still soar above the lake, and the lonesome calls of Canada geese roll across the low prairie. Here, as in all Montana wilderness areas, the denizens of the wild live in fragile harmony with man.

Chapter 6

SELWAY-BITTERROOT
Where people are learning the difference between protecting the forest and perpetuating nature

WHITE CAP CREEK BECKONS beneath a cloudless August sky. Its transparent water dances and tumbles into quiet pools where the dark forms of Chinook salmon once rested after their long journey from the Pacific Ocean. The salmon have all but disappeared, and today most of the shadows crossing the creek's cobblestone bottom fall from tall cedars and ponderosa pines. Sooty scars brand the red-trunked pines as survivors of a recent forest fire—a blaze that left patches of charred snags rising from a mosaic of new green underbrush and tiny pine seedlings. A new generation of forest is sprouting in this scorched corner of the Selway-Bitterroot Wilderness, and with it grows new understanding about fire and its importance to America's wild lands.

This 1,337,910-acre area straddling the Montana-Idaho border refutes one of the most basic ideas about wilderness protection. In the Selway-Bitterroot, foresters are discovering the beneficial role forest fires play in rejuvenating and sustaining the wilderness. Here, as in many of the nation's wilderness areas, people are learning the difference between protecting the land and perpetuating nature.

The wilderness soars above Montana's Bitterroot Valley. The glacier-sculptured Bitterroot Range rises abruptly, its mountains made of granite, gneiss, and schist heaved skyward from deep within the earth. Great east-to-west canyons are gateways that lead high into the mountains, reaching beyond the eastern buttress of the Bitterroots to clusters of small, icy lakes. Dozens of 8,000-foot-plus mountains, including the 10,157-foot Trapper Peak and massive 9,983-foot El Capitan, tower over the rugged landscape. From the Bitterroot Divide, the wilderness drops westward into Idaho, falling thousands of feet to the

Backpackers must climb rugged, trailless country to reach the most remote portions of the Selway-Bitterroot. The many high peaks of the Bitterroot Range are surrounded by steep fields of granite boulders, alpine lakes and cirques, and deep timbered canyons.

wild and scenic Selway River and the Lochsa National Recreation River. Only a narrow road corridor separates the Selway-Bitterroot from Idaho's huge Frank Church–River of No Return Wilderness to the south.

The Selway-Bitterroot's character changes with the terrain. A hot summer dominates the low-lying river canyons of Idaho, where rattlesnakes thrive in the blazing 100°-Fahrenheit temperatures. Elsewhere, dense jungles of lodgepole pine give way to parklike stands of ponderosa. Pockets of spruce and fir lead to scattered alpine larch in the high country. Green meadows, splashed with color by Indian paintbrush, beargrass, and lupine, surround alpine lakes where delicate shooting stars poke their purple heads above muddy shores. In the rocky heights, little else survives but scattered colonies of green and black lichen. Frigid weather grips the wilderness in winter, loosening its hold over the higher elevations for only a few summer weeks.

Large numbers of elk make their home in the timbered canyons and benchlands. Their eerie autumn bugling pierces the wilderness silence, and their hooves carve the only trails that penetrate the Selway-Bitterroot's most remote corners. Elsewhere, human footprints share wilderness trails with the tracks of moose and black bears. Cautious, but curious mule deer investigate the lakeshore camps that disturb their summer range, and silhouettes of brown bats chase swarms of mosquitoes in the night sky. The Selway-Bitterroot is rich in wildlife. In all, 8 varieties of fish, nearly 60 species of mammals, and perhaps 200 different birds inhabit this wilderness.

The Selway-Bitterroot inspired some of the nation's first wilderness-protection efforts. Bob Marshall, who once explored this region, lobbied for its preservation. The Forest Service first set aside portions of the Bitterroot, Lolo, Nezperce, and Clearwater national forests as the Selway-Bitterroot Primitive Area in 1936, and the area was among the

Low-hanging clouds envelop the mountainous interior of the Selway-Bitterroot, left, a land of ever-changing weather. Tiny details of nature's artistry include the curving lines of false hellebore leaves, above left, and the intricate fronds of bracken ferns, above right.

first designated for protection under the Wilderness Act of 1964. Today, the Selway-Bitterroot's boundaries encompass one of the largest wild lands in the country.

But the very act of protecting the Selway-Bitterroot poses a threat to the wilderness. Closure of the area to roads, logging, and other types of development is an essential part of maintaining the Selway-Bitterroot's wilderness character. However, when protecting the area from fire, one of the primary forces of nature, the Forest Service went too far.

For decades, the Forest Service and other government agencies worked quickly to extinguish all wildfires. The goal was simple, the tactics aggressive: control any fire, no matter where, when, or how it started, by 10 a.m. the day after it began. Fire was an enemy attacked by land and air, with pulaskis, axes, bulldozers, and bombers. When protecting commercial timberland, relentless fire-suppression efforts can save precious natural resources. But in places where fire is part of a natural cycle, fire fighting is disruptive. Years ago, some foresters noticed changes in the Selway-Bitterroot. Forests long dominated by ponderosa

A sparsely timbered isthmus, right, separates Mills and Holloway lakes at the northern end of the Bitterroot Range. An alert cow elk, facing page, stares across a rainy meadow for signs of danger. Elk often thrive in the wake of periodic wildfires, which stimulate the growth of browse and create a more diverse forest of different-aged trees. Fires early in the century turned the area into a haven for elk, but the number of animals later declined as people and their fire-fighting tactics prevented fire from playing its essential role.

Bitterroot Range grew worse after settlers arrived in western Montana and began fighting natural fires. Even the Selway-Bitterroot's elk herds have adapted to fire. Elk feed on the brushfields that spring to life in the wake of large fires. Huge fires that burned the area in 1910, 1919, and 1934 created forage for expanding numbers of elk. The brush eventually grew too high for the animals' reach or was crowded out by other plants. Without fire to stimulate growth of new forage, elk numbers began to decline. The Selway-Bitterroot was being altered by man and his attempts to exclude fire.

In the 1940s, a group of foresters suggested allowing fire to play a more natural role in the Selway-Bitterroot. But foresters scrapped the idea after contemplating the public outrage such a policy might produce. The National Park Service in 1968 began allowing some fires to burn in California's Sequoia and Kings Canyon national parks in hopes of restoring natural conditions to high-altitude forests. But in America's wilderness areas, the fight against fire continued.

Fire suppression in the wilderness is a tactic for delaying, not controlling, nature's will. By stopping natural fires from burning, man merely allows forest fuels to build, creating the potential for fires of greater intensity. "Mother Nature is pretty relentless," observes Mick DeZell, fire management officer for the Bitterroot National Forest in Hamilton. "She's going to get it done sooner or later." The Wilderness Act of 1964, the blueprint for America's wilderness-preservation system, calls for protection of areas "affected primarily by the forces of nature, with the imprint of man's work substantially unnoticeable." Foresters read the act, looked at the unmistakable imprint their fire suppression was making on the Selway-Bitterroot, and decided to take another look at the idea of letting fires burn in wilderness.

America's battle against forest fires began in earnest in 1910 after a series of large fires swept through much of western Montana and northern Idaho. It took another fire, burning 63 years later along the Selway-Bitterroot's White Cap Creek, to kindle new ideas about fire and its role in nature.

Two enterprising Forest Service employees, Bob Mutch and Dave Aldrich, hiked into the White Cap drainage in 1970 to begin work on a project that proved fateful: an experiment showing that fire helps, not harms, the wilderness. The two men conducted an exhaustive study of the area and wrote a plan for allowing naturally occurring fires to burn. After their superiors endorsed the plan, they waited for nature to test

were slowly filling in with other species of trees. Wildlife, once abundant, was increasingly hard to find. Insect pests, such as the mountain pine beetle, were spreading farther and faster. People had changed the Selway-Bitterroot with isolated homesteads, decimated salmon runs, and dammed mountain lakes. But these developments were almost insignificant compared to the sweeping effect of fire fighting.

The changes were hardly surprising. The forests here and in much of the northern Rocky Mountains were born of fire. Ponderosa pine, with its thick bark, is especially adapted to periodic fires that clear away the competing understory. Frequent fires also prevent forest litter from accumulating, so there is seldom enough fuel to carry threatening flames to the upper reaches of the tall pines. Most wildfires are small, usually burning one-quarter acre or less. Even the large fires burn in spots and spurts that leave interlaced patches of burned and unburned forest. The result is diversity, an intermingling of old and new growth, of fire-dependent and fire-susceptible vegetation.

Fires help cleanse the forest of pests, such as pine beetles and other insects. One scientific study showed that insect epidemics in the

Colorful moss campion blossoms, above, are part of the diverse wildflower bouquet nature assembles each summer in the Selway-Bitterroot. With its distinctive twin spires, North Trapper Peak, right, is one of the most rugged mountains in the wilderness area.

their theory. The wait ended August 10, 1973, when a bolt of lightning sparked a fire near Fitz Creek, a tributary of White Cap Creek. "The easy decision would have been to go in and put the fire out. That's what we'd been doing," Mutch says. "But that wasn't the right decision." Surrounded by skeptics and fire-horse foresters who described fire with words like *holocaust* and *catastrophe*, the Forest Service watched and waited. The fire burned for 43 days and nights, searing 1,200 acres. In some spots, the blaze wiped out everything; in others it was hard to tell there had been a fire. The fire crawled and smoldered, flared and raged, leaving an irregular pattern in its wake.

The fire brought new life to the White Cap. Blue grouse began feeding in the burned area while smoke was still rising from smoldering logs. After the fire, redstem ceanothus, a favorite elk food, had sprouted at the incredible rate of up to 80,000 seedlings an acre. Before the fire, the area had only scattered clumps of ceanothus. Today, Mutch strides along the White Cap trail and marvels at the change. "I used to fall asleep walking down this trail," he says. "Since the fire, there's something new

A decade after the first major fire was allowed to burn in the White Cap Creek drainage, the Forest Service's Bob Mutch returns to find a lush new forest sprouting beneath a scorched ponderosa pine, right. In August 1984, lightning ignited a 2-acre fire on a ridge overlooking the creek, far right. Most wilderness fires remain small, claiming an occasional tree as they burn irregular patterns along the ground. Whether large or small, fires create areas where new vegetation mingles with old growth timber, adding vital diversity to the forest.

around every bend." He pauses by a large ponderosa and reaches into his knapsack for a faded snapshot. The picture shows the tree, a decade earlier, blackened by fire and surrounded by scorched earth. The tree shows little sign of damage today. The fire scars have nearly healed, and the reddish trunk stands above a carpet of ocean spray and ninebark. "Fire is a process that has sculptured these hills for eons," he says. "Now we're perpetuating a wilderness resource as it should be."

Wilderness scholars and the public were quick to endorse the natural-fire philosophy once it was explained. Sportsmen discovered an increase in elk and other wildlife populations near areas that had burned, and hikers who came to the Selway-Bitterroot enjoyed a wilderness experience in a more natural setting. Lightning-caused fires are now allowed to burn in nearly 9 million acres of national forest wilderness areas, including most of the wildernesses in Montana. Since the 1973 Fitz Creek fire in the Selway-Bitterroot, more than 1,200 separate fires have been allowed to run their course over 190,000 acres of wilderness and national park lands. Yet man has not relinquished all control of the wilderness. Only fires that occur during specified conditions are allowed to burn. If weather and fuel conditions indicate

Part of a timeless wilderness cycle, a tiny Douglas fir seedling grows beneath a blackened stump on a burned-over hillside, left. Fire is a rejuvenating force that has shaped many of the forests of the northern Rockies. By gaining a better understanding about the way fire helps maintain natural conditions, people are learning more about their own role in protecting wilderness. The new ideas have won public approval, but managers still keep close watch on fires. Only blazes occurring under specific conditions are allowed to burn.

that a fire might spread to commercial timberland outside wilderness or that smoke from the fire could create serious pollution in nearby cities, the Forest Service launches its attack. Some foresters now suggest that wilderness fires should be kindled by man under prescribed conditions and not left to the uncertainties of nature. So-called planned ignitions might better control fires and allow wilderness managers to erase the undesirable legacy of decades of overaggressive fire suppression.

New attitudes about fire are just an example of the changing ideas about man's role in the wilderness. Wilderness managers in the Bitterroot National Forest are removing trail registers, not replacing wilderness signs that become damaged or lost, and drastically cutting trail maintenance and construction. A hands-off philosophy of wilderness management is slowly gaining popularity.

A less naive view of man's niche in the wilderness is emerging from the lessons learned along White Cap Creek, a view that reflects a better understanding of what makes wilderness wild. Man cannot control the natural forces that shape wilderness; he can only interfere. Wild places like the Selway-Bitterroot exist not only because they are protected by man, but also because they are protected from him.

Chapter 7

LEE METCALF

An area created by the awesome forces of nature and shaped by the politics of preservation

GLACIERS SCULPTED THE SPECTACULAR peaks of the Lee Metcalf Wilderness. Thundering rivers etched deep canyons in the land. But people, not nature, gave final form to this magnificent region of mountains and meadows. Like all wilderness areas, the Lee Metcalf is largely a product of politics, a place shaped through harsh conflicts and painful compromises.

The 259,000-acre wilderness, located southwest of Bozeman in the Gallatin and Beaverhead national forests, is a case study in the politics of preservation. Haggling men in three-piece suits decided in the distant halls of Congress what natural features to include in the wilderness. The area's boundaries follow negotiated agreements, not the lay of the land. The area is even named for a politician, Montana's late Democratic Sen. Lee Metcalf, an environmental champion who died in 1978.

Jagged 11,000-foot-high peaks of the Madison Range rise from the center of the Lee Metcalf. Fragile alpine basins, dozens of sparkling cirque lakes, and dense lodgepole pine forests surround such mountains as The Helmet, Sphinx Mountain, and Hilgard Peak. Clear streams tumble from the wilderness into the nearby Gallatin and Madison rivers, both nationally famous blue-ribbon trout streams. The Madison River cuts across the northernmost corner of the Lee Metcalf, raging 9 miles through the narrow, 1,500-foot-deep Beartrap Canyon.

The Lee Metcalf is a disjointed, four-part subdivision of what had been until 1983 the largest unprotected expanse of roadless country in the lower 48 states. The southernmost segment, surrounding the gently rounded Monument Mountains, adjoins the northwestern corner of Yellowstone National Park. The main body of the wilderness stretches

Illuminated by morning sunshine, Sphinx Mountain towers above the distant Madison Valley. For many years, the glaciated landscape was ample protection against man's intrusions. Competition for resources turned the area into a political battleground.

northward, spanning the Taylor and Hilgard areas. The two northernmost parcels encompass Beartrap Canyon, near the town of Norris, and the rugged Spanish Peaks, about 25 miles southwest of Bozeman.

Much of the area, especially the portion adjacent to Yellowstone Park, provides critically important habitat for a seriously threatened population of grizzly bears. The Lee Metcalf also supports herds of elk that migrate out of the park in winter, as well as year-round resident populations of elk, moose, and mountain goats. Bighorn sheep thrive in the remote alpine setting, and portions of the area are among the few places in the country where, under a quota system managed by the state Department of Fish, Wildlife and Parks, an unlimited number of sportsmen may hunt the wary sheep. Many of the wilderness lakes and streams contain native and stocked Yellowstone cutthroat trout, along with rainbow, eastern brook, and golden trout.

Spring, summer, and fall are brief interruptions in the long south central Montana winter. West Yellowstone, located a short distance from the Lee Metcalf's southern flank, typically sets record-low temperatures for the nation during the summer. The peaks of the Madison Range remain snowcapped most of the year, although much of the area is snow-free by mid-July. Wilderness trails vary in difficulty from gentle walks to technical mountain climbs, with elevations ranging from 6,000 to more than 11,000 feet. An increasing number of rafters and kayakers are discovering the Madison River in Beartrap Canyon, which contains some of the most challenging rapids in Montana.

The Lee Metcalf is unquestionably wild. But even for the wildest places, protection seldom comes easily. Wilderness designation is a fiercely competitive political process involving carefully planned campaigns, pressure tactics, and sensitive negotiations. More than anything, it takes time.

The Forest Service set aside portions of today's Lee Metcalf as the

Tiny lavender harebell blossoms tremble in the summer breeze. By early summer, heavy snows yield to meadows of green grass and colorful wildflowers. Even in the highest elevations, various flowers bloom until September, when winter reclaims the Lee Metcalf.

Spanish Peaks Primitive Area in 1932. The agency placed a moratorium on development in the Hilgard Peak area in the 1950s, pending a decision on whether to classify it as wilderness, and the Bureau of Land Management later designated Beartrap Canyon a primitive area. With the passage of the Wilderness Act of 1964, speedy wilderness designation, at least for the northern end of the Madison Range, seemed almost certain.

But it took another two decades, several bills in Congress, a congressionally mandated wilderness study, and years of intense political activity to forge the Lee Metcalf Wilderness.

Senator Metcalf tried several times to push a Spanish Peaks wilderness bill through Congress. His early efforts failed because of a sticky landownership problem involving Burlington Northern Incorporated. The railroad holding company owns much of the land in the Gallatin National Forest, its property intermingled in a checkerboard fashion with parcels of national forest.

In the early 1960s, Burlington Northern's predecessor, the Northern Pacific Railway, decided to defer road-building and logging on most of its Madison Range holdings. Company officials had assumed that many of its lands were destined for quick wilderness classification and that the government would buy or trade for the land.

But more than a decade passed without much progress toward wilderness protection for the Madison Range. Meanwhile, an infestation of mountain pine beetles spread through the company's timberlands, killing trees and lowering the value of the land. In 1975, the company asked to trade its 177,000 acres in the Gallatin National Forest for national forest land in western Montana, a deal that could have made wilderness designation for the Lee Metcalf relatively simple. But western Montana loggers, who viewed such a trade as a threat to their supply of public timber, went to Congress for help. Democratic Sen. John Melcher effectively blocked the exchange with a measure requiring congressional approval for any large land trade.

Senator Metcalf successfully sponsored a controversial bill in 1977 requiring the Forest Service to conduct special wilderness studies on several Montana areas, including the Taylor-Hilgard portion of the Madison Range. Despite the study, the area remained in legislative limbo. Finally, in 1978, Burlington Northern managers decided they had waited long enough for Montanans to contemplate the wilderness issue. The company announced plans to build roads across the national forest into its lands in the heart of the Madison Range.

"For 15 years we had sat on our hands," says Don Nettleton of the Plum Creek Timber Company, Burlington Northern's forest products subsidiary. "The status quo was no longer satisfactory." The timber company was sincere in its plan to harvest timber from its land. But at the same time, Nettleton says, it was trying to make a point. "We were pushing the decision," he says. "I'm convinced that there wouldn't be a wilderness area there today if we hadn't made an issue of it."

The threat of roads galvanized Montana environmentalists. An informal group of Bozeman-area residents interested in protecting the mountains near their homes formed the Madison-Gallatin Alliance (MGA) in 1979. Some of the group's early members had worked together on Montana's 1978 anti-nuclear initiative; but for most members, the push for the Lee Metcalf Wilderness was their first experience in the political arena.

Like any political campaign, protecting wilderness requires a solid organization. MGA relied on a hired organizer from the Montana

A miniature forest of moss cradles a drop of rain on a moist rocky ledge high in the Madison Range. Water trickling from alpine icicles, far left, is collected in dozens of clear lakes and streams. Water from rain, melting snow, and wilderness springs eventually finds its way to the Madison or Gallatin rivers, both nationally famous for trout fishing. The pure water produced in the Lee Metcalf feeds tributaries of the mighty Missouri River, which supplies water for irrigation and hydroelectric generation in seven states.

Wilderness Association to get the group started. Much of the organizational work involved the important task of contacting landowners, businessmen, and other groups that might lend support to a wilderness proposal. During the next 3 years, MGA learned the hard way about the importance of having unity in a wilderness campaign.

Conservation groups in 1980 asked the state's congressional delegation to designate a 550,000-acre wilderness extending from the Spanish Peaks to Yellowstone Park, covering portions of the Madison and Gallatin ranges. MGA produced attractive slide shows to win support from Montanans who never had and probably never would visit the wilderness. The group also sponsored marches and demonstrations to call attention to the threat of roads and logging in the pristine area. MGA's leaders effectively used the media to spread information and gain support for the wilderness proposal.

Montana's timber and mining industries staunchly opposed the proposal, as did snowmobile and off-road-vehicle enthusiasts. "We just didn't feel that any more land should be locked up to motorized recreation or natural resource development," says Gary Langley of the Montana Mining Association.

65

The task of settling the issue fell to the state's two representatives and two senators. Because controversies over wilderness designation tend to be local in nature, Congress generally leaves such matters up to politicians from the affected state. Once the state's delegation reaches a consensus, other members of Congress usually go along. With environmentalists asking for more than one-half million acres and industry arguing for none, the delegation began pushing for compromise.

When MGA started making concessions, its organization threatened to disintegrate. Disagreements about boundaries and other issues began pulling apart the pro-wilderness coalition. MGA leaders found themselves at odds with the Montana Wilderness Association as well as with members of their own group. Various factions within the conservation community began lobbying the delegation for different versions of the Lee Metcalf bill. The wilderness advocates lost much of their political clout along with their unity.

"So many people were talking that nobody knew what the hell we stood for," says past MGA President Dr. Richard Tenney.

By late 1982, after years of hearings, discussions, and behind-the-scenes negotiations, the Montana delegation reached a hard-fought agreement on a Lee Metcalf bill. Senator Melcher was hurrying to get the bill approved in the final hours before the 97th Congress adjourned, when Republican Sen. Jesse Helms of North Carolina blocked the measure in retaliation for Melcher's stance on an unrelated agriculture bill. The Lee Metcalf bill died when Congress adjourned without a chance to vote on the measure. The following year, after Melcher introduced another bill, triggering another series of debates and negotiations, the Lee Metcalf became a wilderness.

Politicians consider their wilderness legislation a notable success and a fitting tribute to Metcalf. "We preserved for the future this area as it is," Melcher says. "And we could treat this land no better than that—to say, 'No more change to it because what is here couldn't be improved upon.'"

But the price of such preservation is sometimes high, as Interior Secretary William P. Clark pointed out during a 1984 ceremony dedicating Beartrap Canyon, the nation's first parcel of wilderness to be managed by the Bureau of Land Management. After making his first trip into a wilderness area, Clark told an audience gathered along the banks of the Madison River that "when we are designating a wilderness area, we have to be aware that we're making a major trade-off."

Although Clark was mostly bemoaning the loss of forests for logging and trails for motorcycle riding, his words were an appropriate commentary on the Lee Metcalf. Wilderness protection has become a contest where all sides lose something; nowhere is that clearer than in the Lee Metcalf. Burlington Northern's Nettleton says his company lost financially because pine beetles wiped out much of its Madison Range timber during the long wait for the wilderness issue to be settled. Miners gave up the right to explore the rocky Madison Range for underground wealth, and motorcycle riders accepted another limit to their freedom. But the greatest trade-offs affect the land itself: portions of the Madison Range will be protected for future generations, while equally wild portions will be opened for development.

"It's a disappointment, not a wilderness," says Rick Meis of Bozeman, who helped lead the campaign for the Lee Metcalf. "It's a wilderness compromise."

The wilderness contains fewer than one-half the number of acres conservation groups originally proposed for protection in the Madison and Gallatin ranges. The two southern segments of the wilderness are divided by a wide snowmobile corridor, although special management restrictions there protect important wildlife habitat from development. The Jack Creek drainage, which would have formed a natural link between the northern and southern portions of the wilderness, was traded away to Burlington Northern in exchange for land elsewhere in the Madison Range. One of the greatest concessions made by environmentalists was to exclude from the wilderness Cowboys Heaven, an area between Beartrap Canyon and the Spanish Peaks. With Cowboys Heaven, the Lee Metcalf would have contained dry canyon bottoms, high alpine peaks, and all the land forms in between.

Protecting the Lee Metcalf also exacted a toll on other Montana wilderness areas. The bill designating the area was packed with extraneous amendments, including provisions that opened short corridors for roads into the existing Absaroka-Beartooth and UL Bend wildernesses. Environmentalists' efforts to persuade congressional committees to delete the provisions had little effect other than slowing the bill's passage. Sections of the same bill dropped two roadless areas in eastern and northwestern Montana from consideration as future wilderness.

One environmental activist, outfitter Howie Wolke of Jackson, Wyoming, says the Lee Metcalf is a classic example of an area spoiled by

A 35,000-acre special management area separates the Monument Mountain portion of the wilderness, foreground, from the Taylor-Hilgard portion, on the horizon. The Spanish Peaks area, facing page, features mountains of Precambrian bedrock shaped by glaciers.

politics. A founder of the radical environmental group Earth First!, Wolke faults wilderness advocates for making too many compromises. "They have moved away from confrontation and emotionalism and in a lot of cases have moved across that fine line between working within the system and being co-opted by the system," he says.

Until the early 1970s, most conservation groups steered clear of politics. But in recent years, they have become active participants in the system. When they form a united front, environmentalists present a political force to be reckoned with. "We've demonstrated pretty clearly that there is a force out there," says Carl Pope of the Sierra Club, one of the nation's largest conservation groups. "It's surprising how little it takes to make an impact because not that many people are politically active. Twenty or thirty people in a congressional district are significant. If you can get 100 people, you're a power, a real power."

Much of the political strength environmental groups wield stems from their ability to summon up an amazing amount of volunteer work from dedicated members. "If industry ever spent as much time on this as

environmentalists, who do it out of absolute love for the land, there would never be any wilderness areas," says Joan Montagne, MGA's first president.

Wilderness advocates are still learning, sometimes painfully, how best to use their political muscle. In 1981, a number of Montana's leading conservationists sent Senator Melcher a letter threatening to find an opponent to run against him unless he introduced a satisfactory bill for the Lee Metcalf Wilderness. Although the threat proved idle, close observers say the senator was so angered that environmentalists lost some of their ability to lobby him effectively.

Organizations opposed to wilderness also are becoming more proficient at politics. "We've had mixed luck with the political process in the past, but we're learning how to utilize it better," says Larry Blasing of the timber industry's Inland Forest Resource Council in Missoula. Industry representatives usually talk of wilderness acres in terms of lost jobs and economic harm, words that carry considerable weight in political circles. "Factual economic realities have become a greater concern, and because of that, we're probably having better luck in Congress," Blasing says.

Although wilderness opponents seldom match environmentalists in manpower, they generally do a better job of providing their political candidates with financial support. "You need to support the kind of politician who supports your position, and it takes money to get those folks elected," Blasing says. "That's just the way the system works." The Sierra Club's Pope says environmentalists are becoming more generous with their political contributions, but they need to donate more money. "Many individual members of Congress are responsive to money and not very responsive to grassroots pressure," he says.

Money, power, and politics seem terribly out of place amid the natural beauty and serenity of the wilderness. Fortunately, wilderness politics is like a storm: no matter how hard it rages, it eventually blows over. Today, the protected portions of the Madison Range are a place of solitude where reflected peaks dance on rippled lakes and mountain goats bask in the late-summer sun. The clouds of controversy are at last lifting from the Lee Metcalf as environmentalists, loggers, and politicians move on to other areas to wage new campaigns.

Donna Metcalf warms her wet feet during a Beartrap raft trip. Interior Secretary William Clark, wearing the Stetson, facing page, ended his wilderness tour with a political speech.

Chapter 8

WELCOME CREEK

An undisturbed island in western Montana's vast ocean of roads and logged areas

At FIRST GLIMPSE, the Welcome Creek Wilderness seems undistinguished compared to the grandeur of Montana's flagship wilderness areas. One Forest Service official calls it Montana's mundane wilderness. There are no lakes, no snowy crags, no high cirques, no hanging valleys within its boundaries. Draped down the northeastern slopes of the Sapphire Mountains, Welcome Creek is a relatively small reserve of steep, forested ridges and deep, angular stream courses punctuated by sentinel rock outcrops and low cliffs.

Named for the main watershed that fingers into its upper reaches, this 28,135-acre wilderness provides an enclave of sylvan seclusion amid logging roads and commercial forests that characterize much of the 60-mile-long Sapphire Mountain chain southeast of Missoula. From the spring-fed creek issues pure, cold water that was doubtless welcome enough to the early miners who trekked the surrounding dry summer ridges more than a century ago. The few visitors who find their way up the Welcome Creek canyon today are rewarded with solitude and occasional glimpses of early mining digs, rotting log cabins, and forgotten relics fast disappearing into the undergrowth.

Bounded on the east by Rock Creek, one of the nation's most celebrated blue-ribbon trout streams, the Welcome Creek Wilderness climbs to the crest of the Sapphire Mountains through timbered country of surprising ruggedness. The heart-shaped wilderness area is scarcely 7 miles wide and 10 miles long, yet it challenges even the experienced wilderness explorer. Innocent-looking spur ridges climb with a severity that will impress the most determined hiker. Sloping gently from the top of the range, the ridges soon fall away toward Rock Creek in breaklands

A delicate garden of mushrooms and lichens flourishes on a crumbling log along Welcome Creek, where the wilderness preserves the beauty and serenity of the virgin forest. The pine marten, a cousin of the Russian sable, needs such places to survive.

that give the valley a canyon character even though it is devoid of cliff walls and mantled by forest. From 7,723-foot Welcome Mountain, the highest point in the northern Sapphires, the terrain drops 4,000 feet in less than 5 miles. Hikers climbing Welcome Mountain via the Sawmill Creek trail ascend even faster, climbing 3,000 feet in less than 2.5 miles before gaining the long, luxurious crest of Solomon Ridge.

An important elk summer range, the wilderness also provides undisturbed habitat for pine martens and other wildlife species that require mature forests. Its ridges and canyons are cloaked with a composite of old-growth forests ranging from dry, open Douglas fir slopes to wet spruce bottoms to parklike ridge tops where small, succulent huckleberries flourish under a cool canopy of lodgepole pine. The lower reaches of Welcome Creek support a good fishery of pan-sized cutthroat and other trout. The small creek is almost forgotten next to Rock Creek, with its rich, challenging fishery of rainbow, brook, cutthroat, brown, and Dolly Varden trout, but Welcome Creek provides spawning and rearing areas important to the larger stream.

Welcome Creek was added to the national wilderness system in 1977 after a short, relatively uncontested campaign in which congressional attention focused on more controversial areas where the timber industry sought harvesting rights. Many wondered, before and after, why such an area should be added to a national wilderness system that includes some of the grandest and most scenic of America's public lands. To others who have wandered the Sapphires, with their long, graceful ridges and lodgepole pine parks, the answer is clear.

"Beauty is in the eye of the beholder," quotes one Forest Service manager, explaining Welcome Creek. Defenders of such areas believe the wilderness system has too often been treated as a second national park system, stressing the spectacular "rocks and ice" of the alpine peaks while neglecting the lower undisturbed forests and wildlife habitats that are vanishing most rapidly because of the commodities they can produce.

A decade ago, retired Montana forester William R. "Bud" Moore described the quiet beauty of Welcome Creek in the journals he kept during an autumn and winter spent in an old mining cabin in the heart of the area: "Each intimate twist in the trail—there are many—opened sudden new vistas, mini-worlds they were, each different from the last, expanding ahead then closing behind a giant rock point or spruce tree as I ambled on through the spell of evening hush."

Later, in an informal report to the Missoula district ranger, Moore summed up the essence of the Welcome Creek Wilderness: "In the area's little-disturbed ecosystems lies a rich resource of wildness. Canyon solitude, brawling streams, diverse forests, and their associated wildlife combine to form the wild resource."

The geology of Welcome Creek is typical of the Sapphire Mountains, with rounded ridges of ancient Precambrian seabed rocks that were baked into argillites and quartzites deep in the earth's crust. Some geologists believe the entire range was formed by earth pushed aside when the Idaho batholith welled up more than 70 million years ago to form the Bitterroot Range a dozen miles west. Scattered granitic outcrops in the Welcome Creek Wilderness tell of molten rock injected from below, creating both the small pockets of gold that lured the early miners and the scattered sapphire deposits 50 miles south that give the mountain range its name. Dark granitic rocks loom along Rock Creek at the Dalles, near the mouth of Welcome Creek, where a suspension footbridge spans Rock Creek at the main wilderness entrance. Other granites occur near the top of 7,240-foot Cleveland Mountain, on the western rim of the wilderness, where the Cleveland Mine once worked an underground vein.

Gold was first discovered in Welcome Creek in 1888, and the early pick-and-shovel miners quickly extracted most of it from "placer" or streambed pockets eroded from higher veins. The mining boom revived in 1895, with news of gold strikes just across the Rock Creek canyon on Quigg Peak. A town known as Quigley sprang up on the northeastern edge of the Welcome Creek Wilderness, opposite Sawmill Creek, and promoters secured $1.5 million in backing from speculators whose ranks

Tumbling through an area of subtle beauty, Welcome Creek is a fount of pure water for Rock Creek, a blue-ribbon trout stream that flows along the area's eastern boundary.

72

included President Grover Cleveland. But the boom ended abruptly when investors learned that the discovery was a fraud.

The Welcome Creek mining era was brief, but according to one local historian it yielded one of the largest nuggets ever found in the state, one that must have approached 1.5 pounds and would have brought about $10,000 on today's market. Somehow it escaped official record. In all, Welcome Creek yielded only about $30,000 in gold, at turn-of-the-century prices. Several mining claims remained active through 1983, but none proved promising enough to justify development. The claims expired with the end of the 19-year grace period the Wilderness Act mandated for miners.

When the mines were abandoned in about 1900, lower Rock Creek briefly became a haunt for outlaws and horse thieves, notably one Frank Brady, who was pursued during the summer of 1904 and finally killed in a Thanksgiving Day shoot-out at an old Welcome Creek cabin. Thereafter, the Welcome Creek country slumbered for 60 years until the Forest Service pushed a logging road into the upper flanks of Welcome Mountain in the mid-1960s, at a cost of $90,000. Major clearcuts were mapped out across the Welcome Creek headwaters, and the timber harvest rights were sold in 1969. When the Forest Service inventoried its potential wilderness lands in 1971, Welcome Creek was overlooked. Conservation groups, worried about potential impacts of roads and logging on Rock Creek, filed a broad appeal questioning government logging plans for the Rock Creek watershed. The action led to formation of the Rock Creek Advisory Council, an unprecedented citizen advisory group with a federal mandate to help the Forest Service redraw its plans in order to protect the watershed. The council included ranchers, miners, sportsmen, businessmen, and representatives from conservation groups and the timber industry. All agreed that watershed protection should be the top priority in the drainage.

Meanwhile, sportsmen took new interest in Welcome Creek when a landmark Montana elk and logging study began documenting the animal's habits in the northern Sapphires and a half-dozen other parts of the state. The purpose was to learn more about how logging affects elk habits. Inadvertently, researchers discovered that Welcome Creek is a favorite summer haunt and migration route for many of the roughly 300 elk that winter on the state's Threemile Game Range, in the western foothills of the Sapphires.

By 1977, Welcome Creek had been proposed in Congress as a

Trails of grueling steepness climb the forested ravines and ridges of Welcome Creek Wilderness. Peaks of the Rattlesnake Mountains are visible from the top of the Sapphires.

wilderness area. Conservation groups, pressing for a new inventory of roadless lands, cited it to illustrate the shortcomings of the first one. Time and economics had caught up with the Welcome Creek timber sale, which had been extended three times, transferred from one company to another, and reduced in size. When its transfer to a third firm was proposed, the Forest Service canceled the sale, and wilderness designation quickly followed.

Though mundane to some, Welcome Creek offers a glimpse of the Sapphire Mountains as they were before modern management. Moore views it as "a major island in an ocean of roads and logged areas." It may turn out to be a scientific treasure for future foresters interested in measuring the long-term changes that logging and management produce on tree growth, soil fertility, wildlife diversity, watershed protection, and evolutionary change. A system of natural research areas is taking shape in Montana to fill the scientific gap, but the areas are small and scattered. Some believe there should be a representative wilderness area like Welcome Creek in every mountain range in the state.

Chapter 9

ANACONDA-PINTLER

A mountainous area where the future of wilderness resources rests with skilled managers

SOLITUDE ENRICHES THE GRANDEUR of the windswept ridges, alpine meadows, and forested valleys of the Anaconda-Pintler Wilderness. At the 9,498-foot summit of West Pintler Peak, signs of humanity are as innocuous as the small brass marker that records where the U.S. Geological Survey measured the summit elevation. Yet the unseen hands of man affect the wilderness daily—managing its resources, changing the habits of visitors, and directing the ever-growing amount of recreation traffic in hopes of protecting the area's wild qualities.

Wilderness is decried by some people as a lockup of valuable resources—areas set aside for the recreational pleasure of a few at the expense of all others. In reality, the land remains productive. Wilderness precludes only one of the five broad multiple uses of the national forests: commercial timber production. Other renewable resources—watershed, livestock forage, wildlife, and recreation—are the dominant ones in a wilderness area, and they, too, require management.

The phrase *wilderness management* may strike some as a contradiction in terms. In a place where man's influence is supposed to be substantially unnoticeable, managing wilderness might seem unwarranted. But in today's world, wilderness is not always able to take care of itself.

"At the time a lot of these areas were set aside, public use was light," says George Stankey of Missoula, a Forest Service researcher specializing in wilderness management. "The areas were remote, and many of the management tasks were taken care of by the remoteness. There just wasn't the pressure." But the situation has changed. Growing public use of wilderness areas has increased pressure in the past two decades, and

West Pintler Peak dwarfs a lone hiker near the Continental Divide in the Anaconda-Pintler. The boundaries of four counties and three national forests converge at the peak. Cooperation among various interests is key to managing the area as an enduring resource.

every new visitor leaves some mark on the land.

The Wilderness Act directs agencies to preserve the wild qualities of the land as an enduring resource—a directive that requires federal land managers to take appropriate action to protect the wilderness. In most instances, however, "wilderness management" might be more accurately called "people management."

Public attention usually focuses on the issue of wilderness designation, but many people believe that management of the areas is of equal or greater importance. "Getting lines drawn around an area is only part of the task," Stankey says. "Unless we start seeing more and more attention on management, a lot of the energy devoted to wilderness allocation might be all for naught."

The Anaconda-Pintler Wilderness illustrates many of the challenges facing contemporary wilderness managers. Located southwest of Butte, the wilderness straddles the Anaconda Range, a geological anomaly where the Continental Divide doubles back on itself in an east-west crescent nearly 80 miles long around the northern end of the Big Hole Valley. Along the western arm of the crescent, the earth has hurled up 10,000-foot peaks in a mountain range where the young granites of the Idaho and Boulder batholiths press against ancient Precambrian mudstones and gray limestones of the Madison Formation.

Named for pioneer Big Hole rancher Charles Ellsworth Pintler and for the historic copper-smelting town of Anaconda on its eastern end, the Anaconda-Pintler Wilderness contains 159,086 acres extending more than 30 miles along the great Divide. It receives only moderate use. A rancher who lives nearby calls it Montana's forgotten wilderness.

Like most wilderness mountain ranges, the rugged Anacondas form a geographical barrier that dictates human custom. Separating the sprawling ranches of the Big Hole from the Deer Lodge and Bitterroot valleys, the formidable terrain of the Anaconda Range has been a

Phyllis Lakes form part of the headwaters of the Middle Fork of Rock Creek. Besides producing water for distant farms and cities, the area provides habitat for wildlife and forage for livestock. Managing such resources requires cooperation among agencies.

natural division for political jurisdictions and land management agencies. The boundaries of four counties and three national forests wander along the Divide and thread down the major ridges and drainages.

The wilderness is high country. With the exception of a few stream valleys, all of the land is above 7,000 feet in elevation and is locked in snow more than half the year. Mountain goats live in the area year-round, but the elk and deer that spend summers in the wilderness migrate to lower elevations in winter.

Historically, the area has been fringe territory, easily forgotten and left alone by managers who were preoccupied with the social demands of the settled valleys and with the timber and livestock forage that the more productive foothills can produce. The designation of wilderness areas within such rugged zones reflects the new public interest in those wild areas in this era when such places are fast disappearing.

That interest places new management demands on district rangers and forest supervisors, whose jobs are made more difficult when a wilderness is broken into different jurisdictions separated by great distances. Management of the Anaconda-Pintler Wilderness is divided among the Deerlodge, Bitterroot, and Beaverhead national forests and five ranger districts, four of which play an active role.

The tasks associated with wilderness management are intended to protect the area's wilderness qualities. Trails must be maintained or rebuilt periodically to allow reasonably easy access to hikers and horsemen while limiting damage to the surrounding land. Public education is becoming an increasingly important responsibility for managers. In popular areas, rangers check outfitter and visitor camps, often teaching people how to enjoy the wilderness without harming it. Seemingly small jobs, such as posting signs or revising maps, are essential in directing people away from problem areas.

Other management work is aimed more at wilderness resources than people. Grazing allotments and range conditions must be monitored, along with forest insects, diseases, and fires. Bridges and water diversions are sometimes necessary for reducing trail erosion. Historical sites and unusual plant and animal species must be safeguarded. As with most government activities, extensive record keeping is required for everything.

The work is guided by a management plan completed in 1977. The plan, drafted by rangers with advice from the public, lists 16 broad goals for protecting the wilderness. The goals range from maintaining natural diversity and populations of fish and wildlife to establishing consistent management practices throughout the wilderness. But with tight federal budgets limiting the amount of money for wilderness management, many of the goals have proved elusive.

During fiscal year 1984 in the Forest Service's Northern Region, which includes more than 5 million acres of wilderness in five states, the agency spent about $1 million for wilderness management and $2 million for trail maintenance and reconstruction. Only a fraction of that money found its way to projects in the Anaconda-Pintler Wilderness. In part, the expenditures reflect the general scarcity of federal money. But the budgets are also an indication of government priorities.

In the Forest Service, management of timber receives top priority, largely because timber sales produce revenue for the national treasury. Programs such as wilderness management and recreation receive less attention and funding because they contribute little money to federal coffers. In the Anaconda-Pintler, the four ranger districts that share responsibility for the area spent $41,479 or 1.6 percent of their combined budgets on wilderness management in 1984. Those same ranger districts spent $1.36 million—54 percent of their budgets—on timber management during the same period.

Rangers are using better planning and cooperation among the widely scattered ranger districts as a positive step toward making the dwindling money stretch further. Managers meet twice a year to coordinate trail work and discuss problems. They also bring all the trail crews together once a year to pool their efforts on a major trail or bridge reconstruction job.

Cooperation also has helped along the Divide, where one of the more complete sections of the proposed Continental Divide Trail traverses the length of the wilderness. As the trail crosses and recrosses the Divide, it drifts in and out of different ranger districts. Use of the trail is starting to increase, and joint trail projects are improving sections where it is difficult to follow.

Wilderness management also involves other agencies, some of which play a crucial role. Fish and wildlife, for example, are under the state's purview. Fishing is popular in the wilderness and draws heavy use around certain lakes. Many of the 42 fishable lakes in the Anaconda Range were once barren, but stocking since 1932 has populated them with rainbow and cutthroat trout. State stocking decisions can be a potent management tool for changing visitor habits. Fishermen are more likely to camp alongside a lake filled with trout than one that is barren. By stocking fish in one lake rather than another, managers are in effect redirecting people.

Sometimes, work necessary for sound wilderness management is conducted independently by naturalists whose motivation is scientific curiosity and a love for the wilds. For example, the Forest Service has done little to identify rare plants and plant communities in the wilderness. But Klaus Lackschewitz, retired assistant curator for the University of Montana Botany Department, spent 10 years studying the flowers of the Anaconda-Pintler Wilderness, cataloging hundreds of species. The wilderness plan calls for encouraging private research, but there is no guarantee that managers will learn of independent studies or put them to work. Without such studies, it is often difficult to watch for changes or protect critical sites.

To stretch budgets, rangers have turned to volunteer help. Students from as far away as Sweden have worked as wilderness guards or trail crew members. The trend, which extends beyond the Anaconda-Pintler,

A rare combination of granitic and argillitic soils in the Anaconda Range supports an unusual diversity of wildflowers, including the alpine forget-me-not. A circumpolar species found also in Norway and Switzerland, the delicate flower is a relic of an age when the earth's continents were joined. Other flowers include the extremely rare Saussurea weberii, *which has a showy silver, blue, and white blossom. The flower often cited as the rarest in the Anacondas,* Penstemon lemhiensis, *actually grows outside the wilderness.*

is starting to displace veteran seasonal workers. Concerned about both their job security and the quality of work done by volunteers, many wilderness rangers and trail crewmen have formed a Backcountry Workers' Association to lobby for better wildland management and better opportunity for experienced workers.

With so much wilderness work still undone, some managers wonder whether their goals are too ambitious. Others believe that certain areas of heavy use are bound to become sacrifice areas, where wilderness pilgrims will exact a toll for leaving the rest of the wilderness alone.

Some management goals can probably be deferred in the Anaconda-Pintler, where use remains relatively light. But other long-range tasks, such as collecting baseline information on water quality and public use, will be crucial to rangers trying to watch for critical changes in the future. Paradoxically, the lure of wilderness adventure that leads to overuse and abuse of the land may also engender the public support necessary to bolster wilderness management. The skill of wilderness managers may well determine whether wilderness areas will endure as lasting examples of a world beyond the influence of man or linger briefly as the last islands to yield to the human tide.

Chapter 10

GATES OF THE MOUNTAINS

An alluring vestige of America's frontier, where vicarious explorers outnumber visitors

WHERE THE NORTHERN END of the Big Belt Mountain Range shoulders toward the Rocky Mountain front, the Missouri River has carved a deep gorge through layers of sedimentary rock on the northeastern edge of the broad Helena Valley.

"Every object here wears a dark and gloomy aspect," Meriwether Lewis wrote in July 1805 as the Lewis and Clark expedition made its way up the Missouri. "The river appears to have forced its way through this immense body of solid rock . . . and where it makes its exit below has thrown on either side vast columns of rocks mountains high."

Lewis called it the Gates of the Rocky Mountains. Viewed from the summer tour boats that ply the gorge, the rocky columns seem to blend together, closing like gates until it is difficult to see where the broad river flows from the gorge.

High above the canyon, the 28,500-acre Gates of the Mountains Wilderness basks atop the northern end of the Big Belts as one of Montana's smallest, least visited, yet most alluring wilderness areas. Wild canyons wind up through limestone formations weathered into spires, cliffs, twisting outcrops, and graceful, thin walls. Above the canyons, long timbered ridges wander among forested peaks, rocky outcrops, and gentle mountain meadows and solitary springs. Well-kept trails climb gradually into the wilderness through forests of ponderosa pine and Douglas fir, the open, parklike forest floor contrasting sharply with the dense undergrowth of many other wilderness forests.

Set aside as a primitive area in 1949, the Gates of the Mountains became a wilderness in 1964. Challenging, but not formidable, the area is nearly ideal for a first trip into a wilderness. Yet it is lightly used,

Simply knowing that wild places exist, over the ridge or beyond the next turn, gives some people an appreciation of wilderness. Relatively few hikers explore the Gates of the Mountains, yet thousands of visitors gaze in each year from the Missouri River below.

showing few impacts even at popular spots. Most visitors prefer to experience it as Lewis and Clark did, from the river far below.

In 1983, nearly 27,000 visitors cruised the river to ponder the limestone formations, watch mountain goats high on the canyon cliffs, and enjoy the wilderness vicariously from the tour boats operated by Gates of the Mountains Incorporated. Most of them probably had little ambition to hike up the steep canyons when the boat stopped at Meriwether Campground. They were content simply to know that a vestige of wild America had been preserved for future generations as habitat for wildlife and as a link with America's frontier past.

Experts say that vicarious users are now the largest group of wilderness supporters, outnumbering those who actually visit the areas. Some have made a trip or hope to make one in the future, but most experience the wilderness through books, photographs, or stories told by friends. For them, it is not necessary to travel through the wilds to value them. Some suggest that in a world overrun by humans, perhaps there should be wilderness areas where people are not allowed at all.

In the Gates of the Mountains Wilderness, nature has imposed one severe limit that helps discourage visitors: except for brief periods in spring and fall, the land is arid. Spring comes early to the Gates, by Montana mountain standards. In a normal year, all but the highest forests are free of snow by mid-May. Porous, limestone soils quickly absorb the winter snowmelt, and the natural springs and streams of the wilderness come alive. The land greens as wildflowers blossom along the trails and spread across the high meadows. Among them is a rare member of the rose family, *Kelseya uniflora,* a striking heathlike shrub that clings to the limestone cliffs and stony summits in mounds and is found only in a few parts of Montana and Idaho on the Madison Limestone Formation. Pink blossoms of a tiny primrose, *Douglasia Montana,* also adorn the high ridges in great profusion. Another unusual

Limestone cliffs rise steeply above Willow Creek, one of the four main drainages in the Gates. A scarcity of water deters many hikers during the hot summer months. The Beartooth Game Management Area, beyond the ridge, is just north of the wilderness.

flower, it grows only in Montana's central mountains and parts of British Columbia and northern Wyoming.

By early July, streams disappear underground, and springs that flowed earlier become infrequent and unreliable. The canyons bake under the hot summer sun. For all but the most determined, the hiking season ends. The few hardy summer visitors must pack their own water at 8.3 pounds a gallon. Fall rains replenish the water and bring new life to the high springs, just in time for the hunting season. The Gates is a popular hunting area—too popular for many of the more experienced hunters—and it supports healthy numbers of elk, bighorn sheep, mountain goats, mule deer, and blue grouse. Black bear also inhabit the wilderness, as do bobcats and mountain lions.

Elk from the Big Belts gather in winter just north of the wilderness in the state's 32,000-acre Beartooth Game Management Area, which also has a large resident elk herd. A grass-and-timber foothills region, it was a major cattle ranch until 1971. Bighorn sheep and mountain goats are also scattered across the northern end of the wilderness, from the Willow and Porcupine creek drainages to the steep hills and cliffs along the Missouri River canyon, where they are often visible from the river tour boats. Sheep also range over the upper slopes of Candle Mountain.

Sheep, goats, and elk were hunted to extinction in the Big Belts and many other places by the early 1900s, by a generation of hunters who naively viewed wildlife as an unlimited resource requiring no management or protection. State game managers began re-establishing the goats in the 1940s with surplus animals brought from the Bob Marshall Wilderness and its adjoining Deep Creek country. Elk from Yellowstone National Park were added in the 1950s, as were sheep from the Bob Marshall's Sun River Canyon.

Bob Cooney, a retired state game manager long interested in the Gates, recounts how goats were trapped at a natural salt lick in the Bob Marshall, floated down a wilderness river in crates on 12-man rubber rafts, and then flown to Helena from a primitive airstrip for the final pickup truck ride to their new home. All survived.

Rocky limestone formations turn the wilderness canyons into mysterious miniature badlands whose side gulches and steep coulees invite exploration. Shadows of overhanging ledges and deep grottoes accent the escarpments and palisades, though no full-fledged caves have been discovered. Geologists say the strange formations were fashioned from stone originally deposited as marine sediments on the bed of an ancient warm, shallow sea. Similar deposits may be forming today beneath the Gulf of Mexico. Uplifted along with the Big Belts, the limestone zone was sculpted into intricate swirls and spires as erosion gradually carved the mountain stream courses. The gray limestones mingle with the tans and umbers of shale, especially near the rounded, timbered summit of 7,980-foot Moors Mountain, the highest point in the wilderness, and on the exposed flanks of nearby 7,443-foot Candle Mountain, where fossilized shells are embedded in the higher rocks. Visible from Helena, Candle Mountain was named a century ago when a forest fire burned to the top, causing the summit to glow for days like a distant candle. Gnarled, ghostly snags mingle with five-needled limber pines along Candle's long ridge top, but most of the arid southern face still remains barren of trees.

Fires have left their mark on the dry forests in many parts of the Gates of the Mountains. On August 5, 1949, a disastrous forest fire

turned into a human tragedy when afternoon winds whipped lightning-caused flames into an inferno in Mann Gulch, just northeast of the wilderness. The blaze was intercepted by a recreation guard from Meriwether Campground and by 16 Forest Service smokejumpers, most of them fighting their first major fire. Turbulent canyon winds suddenly carried the fire down the gulch, cutting off their retreat. The men panicked and scattered when their foreman tried to start a "backfire" to create a burned island of safety ahead of the advancing flames. The foreman's plan worked, and he survived, but only two others outran the flames in their final desperate race back up the punishingly steep canyon. The fire prompted a major investigation, and the memory of the tragedy lives on whenever Montana foresters recount the litany of the state's great forest fires.

The wilderness climate—so vulnerable to fire and discouraging to summer visitors—creates a solitude that can draw interest from odd quarters. One wilderness manager relates how the Gates of the Mountains was recommended in a men's magazine in the late 1970s in response to a reader's inquiry about seldom-visited wilderness areas where discreet nude backpacking might be possible. The following season, an astonished trail crew reported meeting a couple who were hiking down the trail wearing nothing but shoes and backpacks.

Roadless lands south of the wilderness contribute to its isolation and make it effectively larger. A proposed 10,000-acre wilderness addition is expected to win early approval. It will move the southern boundary of the Gates to within a quarter-mile of the Beaver Creek Road to include Refrigerator Canyon, a natural wonder where cool winds blow even in summer beneath cliffs hundreds of feet high that narrow to a gunsight gorge scarcely 10 feet wide at the bottom. Still, the vast majority of visitors will probably continue to view the wilderness only from the Missouri River canyon, as they have since pioneer rancher Nicholas Hilger first began the river boat tours in 1890. Wild and alluring, the Gates of the Mountains represents wilderness at its finest, enjoyed by most from a distance and spared from heavy human impacts.

May sunshine brings a burst of color to the wilderness as clumps of Douglasia Montana, *a tiny primrose, blossom along the high open ridges below Candle Mountain.*

Chapter 11

MISSION MOUNTAINS

A place to rediscover the spirit of wildness, a link to a heritage fast disappearing

THE BOLD PEAKS OF THE MISSION Mountains crown a wilderness range unique in the West both in majesty and management. Soaring more than a mile above the farms and villages of the Mission Valley, the austere western front of the Missions forms one of the most striking mountain valleys in the Rockies.

But the range is more than a natural wonder. It is the first place in America in which an Indian nation has matched the federal government in dedicating tribal lands as a wilderness preserve. The Mission Mountains are two wilderness areas in one, divided along the crest of the range by the boundary of the Flathead Indian Reservation. East of the Mission divide, the Flathead National Forest manages 73,877 acres of wild country under the Wilderness Act of 1964. West of the divide, 89,500 acres have been set aside as a tribal wilderness by the Confederated Salish and Kootenai (Flathead) Tribes. Both wilderness areas are managed cooperatively and are open to everyone, but subtle differences in management style reflect tribal needs and traditions. For example, hunting in the tribal wilderness is reserved for tribal members, for whom it remains important both as a food source and as a link with tribal heritage.

The imposing western front of the Missions seems to reveal the wilderness peaks, basins, and headwalls in every detail; instead, it masks the true extent of an area 30 miles long and 6 to 10 miles wide. Trails of punishing steepness climb to hidden basins, big lakes, glaciated hanging valleys, and secret mountain passes. Delicate alpine flowers tremble in the wind atop broad ridges guarded by flanks so steep they defy human approach.

Relentless winds weave tendril patterns on the snowfields that mantle McDonald Peak, highest point in the Mission Mountains Wilderness. Named for early fur trader Angus McDonald, the glacier-studded mountain crests the nation's first Indian wilderness.

A dozen peaks over 9,000 feet rise from the southern end of the Missions, dominated by the great snowy head of 9,820-foot McDonald Peak. The tall central crest of the range catches the prevailing westerly winds, wringing down more than 100 inches of annual moisture, most of it snow. Alpine snowfields linger year-round, feeding a half dozen named glaciers and melting into icy streams and springs that purl through a remarkable 350 lakes, ponds, and pools.

Waterfalls are numerous. Mission Falls, cascading 600 feet down a rocky headwall in the shadow of the Garden Wall, is a landmark above the historic mission village of St. Ignatius. Most of the wilderness lakes were originally barren, cut off from migrating trout by steep rushing streams and falls that posed formidable natural barriers. Many high lakes freeze out in winter, but during the past 50 years trout have been established in about half of the more than 100 larger lakes. Native cutthroat predominate, but some lakes offer rainbow, brook, and even golden trout.

Elk, once famous for their trophy size in the central Missions, still inhabit much of the wilderness, notably the southwestern end. Goats are widespread, and a small band of bighorn sheep was introduced in North Crow Creek Canyon in 1979. Although hunting in the tribal wilderness is limited to tribal members, fishing and other wilderness activities are permitted for non-members who hold valid tribal recreation permits. State hunting and fishing licenses are also required.

An estimated 25 grizzly bears still range the Missions, and tribal managers place a high priority on their protection. Each summer, amid the snowfields and glaciers of McDonald Peak, the Mission grizzlies rendezvous in one of nature's enigmatic cycles of life. Ladybugs and cutworm moths congregate by the thousands, perhaps emerging from hibernation or drawn together for reproduction. The grizzlies migrate to the mountain summit to feed on insects, and some bears linger near the

cool snowfields for most of the summer. Concerned that the spectacle might draw curiosity-seekers, tribal managers have closed a 12,000-acre area around the mountain from mid-June through September. Signs posted at trailheads and strategic mountain passes warn visitors to respect the closure, and tribal managers patrol to ensure compliance. Biologists monitor the bears from an observation post on a nearby mountain.

In the eastern Missions, the Forest Service has imposed more-limited closures around the shores of heavily used Glacier and Cold lakes, where camps and fires are no longer welcome, due to impacts from past use. Fishing and day use are permitted.

Tribal managers still experiment with stocking fish in some lakes, and they occasionally use helicopters to shuttle supplies or track wildlife. They also have a more vigorous program for patrolling closures and checking popular trails. To help support management, the tribal government sells recreational use permits to non-members for $10 a year. A permit entitles the holder to hike, fish, camp, and enjoy most other recreational pursuits on tribal lands.

By contrast, the Forest Service has been reducing its wilderness presence in response to tighter federal budgets. Use fees have not been proposed, because of resistance from a public that believes it already supports wilderness management with its taxes. In 1983, no wilderness ranger was assigned to the Missions. In 1984, the agency decided to contract with the private sector for wilderness field work. A former seasonal wilderness ranger won the contract. The work includes clearing trails blocked by fallen trees, answering visitor questions, cleaning up litter, and instructing campers how to reduce their impacts. Some see the move toward contracting as a disturbing precedent that will further separate desk-bound foresters from the land they manage. Others believe it will help contain costs and reduce the bureaucracy.

The Forest Service maintains 71 miles of trail, and 45 miles climb the tribal portion of the Missions. Most are difficult for horse travel, which is discouraged to reduce competition with wildlife for the limited food available in the high country. The tortuous switchback trail up Post Creek, known as the "angel's staircase," is so severe that every year or two an unseasoned packhorse bolts and plunges to its death. The trail was closed for a week in 1983 due to the danger that one such carcass might attract grizzly bears. Unable physically to remove the carcass, tribal managers ultimately wrapped it with 100 pounds of spaghetti gel

Game wardens and biologists measure and tag a grizzly family relocated in 1983 after the bears strayed from the wilderness. Such efforts have helped reduce the number of grizzlies killed by landowners.

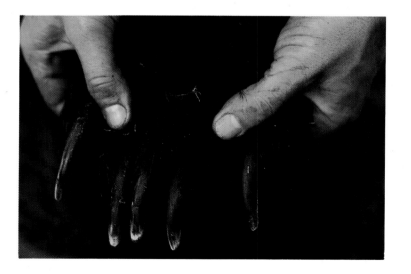

Serrated edges of 9,001-foot Gray Wolf Peak, facing page, divides tribal wilderness and national forest on the southern flank of the Missions. Above, only narrow Swan Valley separates the silhouetted Missions from Holland Peak in the Bob Marshall.

explosive and blasted it into oblivion.

The Mission Mountains Wilderness is rich in lore, much of it related to the Salish and Kootenai tribes. Like other Indians, they are heirs to a culture buffeted by outside encroachment and misunderstanding. Explorers Lewis and Clark called them Flatheads, but many tribal members insist today that their forefathers were mistaken for another tribe farther west whose members cosmetically flattened their foreheads. A peaceful people, the Flatheads were often raided by warlike tribes as they crossed the wilderness mountains to hunt buffalo on the Montana Plains to the east. Today, a few tribal elders can still trace the routes of old hunting trails that crossed the Mission Mountains. The wilderness mountains also held vision-quest sites, places still considered sacred, where young tribal members would fast alone and wait for a spiritual vision to guide them in later life. Other spots were summer camps where families gathered berries, roots, and medicinal plants. As white settlers arrived and the Indians were confined to the reservation, oldtime Missions outfitter Bud Cheff says, some trails were built as escape routes or travel ways for guerrilla wars of resistance that never came.

Opening of the reservation to homesteading coincided with development of the Flathead Irrigation Project and construction of dams that created reservoirs and enlarged existing lakes along the western foot of the mountains.

In the early 1920s, Theodore Shoemaker of the Forest Service led railway parties and mountaineering groups on exploration trips into the Missions. The trips inspired the first map of the area, along with many of the lyrical names given to Mission landmarks: Lake of the Stars, Lake of the Clouds, Sunrise Glacier, Picture Lake, Daughter of the Sun Mountain, and Turquoise Lake. Other names, such as Mount Harding and McDonald Peak, leave some tribal members dissatisfied and may ultimately be abandoned in favor of Indian names.

In 1931, the eastern Missions became a Forest Service primitive area, and in 1936, the Flathead Tribal Council resolved to make the western Missions an Indian national park. But the park idea was stalled in Washington, D.C., where early wilderness advocate Bob Marshall was working for the Bureau of Indian Affairs to set aside wild areas on Indian reservations. Eventually he established 16 of them, but 15, including the Missions, were later declassified by tribes resentful of such federal intervention. Wyoming's Wind River Reservation still has a wilderness, but the Flathead tribes take pride in having set aside the Missions on their own terms.

The edges of the wilderness contain a few areas that some believe could produce commercial timber. Logging has occurred inside the wilderness on low-lying tribal, Forest Service, and former railroad lands. The old Northern Pacific Railway once owned 30 percent of the eastern Missions, although the land was gradually exchanged for other forest land outside the wilderness. The Forest Service wilderness today includes about 2,000 acres logged under special authorization in the 1950s to salvage insect-killed timber. Logging has been proscribed since the Forest Service primitive area became a wilderness in 1964, but it is still a possibility within the tribal wilderness.

Tribal member Thurman Trosper, a former top Forest Service official, became the prime mover for the tribal wilderness in 1975 after his retirement. The Tribal Council endorsed the idea and retained the University of Montana's Wilderness Institute to study suggested boundaries and draft a management plan for the area. The final plan, which

was drafted by David Rockwell, was adopted by the council in 1981 when the Mission Mountains Tribal Wilderness became a reality.

A past national president of the Wilderness Society, Trosper has wandered the Missions since he was a teenager. He resolutely opposes scarring the face of the Missions with permanent roads, but, living on a reservation where jobs are scarce, he is mindful of the potential value of the 4 million board feet per year of timber the edges of the tribal wilderness could yield.

"An Indian wilderness is not a federal wilderness," he notes, adding that the tribes still "have the option to take timber." Horse-loggers cleared the lower slopes of the Missions in the early 1920s on North Crow Creek, but the scars healed in the relatively stable argillitic soils of the Missions. He believes careful horse-logging may still be an option in the wilderness. Logging on other tribal lands is an economic mainstay for the roughly 3,000 tribal members who live on the reservation. An equal number have left to find jobs elsewhere. The Flatheads are a minority both on their reservation and in their wilderness. Out of 4,000 wilderness visitors in summer 1977, only 5 percent were Indian.

Some management issues reach beyond the wilderness boundary, a dilemma illustrated by the Mission grizzlies. Most wilderness areas protect only scenic, high alpine country and contain few lowlands. Forested foothills and valley lands are excluded because they lack spectacular scenery and are valued for timber production, farmland, or subdivision. But the austerity of the high mountains limits survival for animals just as it does for humans. The grizzly hibernates and summers in alpine country but in the spring and fall descends to valley stream bottoms, where food is more plentiful.

Today grizzly feeding areas are limited on both sides on the Missions. To the east, in the Swan River Valley, timber sales and valley farmsteads are expanding inexorably, although managers try to balance the bears' need for cover with timber harvests that may increase the forage plants used by the bears. Only one or two timbered travel corridors remain across the valley to link the Mission bears with the larger grizzly population roaming the Bob Marshall Wilderness complex.

Along the western front of the Missions, where timbered stream bottoms thread out among farms and ranches, the problem is more dramatic. Grizzlies descend along the stream bottoms, venturing 3 to 4 miles out into the valley. They often sleep by day in the secluded stringers of timber and thick brush, making nocturnal grazing forays into

Thriving atop the Missions, subalpine buttercups and white cushion phlox, above, adorn the rocky heights. The tiny blossoms accentuate the immensity of Daughter-of-the-Sun Mountain, facing page, flanked left and right by Turquoise and Lost lakes.

surrounding croplands. Attractive nuisances, such as old orchards, garbage dumps, or livestock carcasses, may draw them to farmsteads. A newcomer's streamside home in the trees may turn out to be in the middle of a grizzly travel route. Some residents have been unnerved by the sight of a half dozen mammoth bears padding silently across a corral by moonlight or through a farmyard in the glow of a yard light.

Grizzlies have rarely killed livestock. More often, bears fall victim to landowners' fears. Between 1976 and 1982, at least 13 Mission grizzlies were killed—a dramatic loss for an area that may have a stable population of only 25 bears. Reproduction may not cover such losses, so managers are trying to intervene more rapidly to avert problems. In 1983, a large female and two cubs were trapped by tribal, state, and federal managers and moved to the Great Bear Wilderness after a farmer complained that they were feeding on a sheep carcass. The mother, dubbed Daisy, had been trapped before and had no history of mischief. It was not certain that she had killed the sheep. But managers now strive to relocate any bears that seem too familiar with humans or

Tribal resource manager Fred Matt scales the towering Garden Wall, where alpine flowers and snow cornices share a broad ridge top.

livestock. The strategy may be paying off. Since 1980, only four grizzlies have been killed, while six others have been trapped and relocated.

Despite relocation efforts, bears often return to their home ranges. They are capable of traveling great distances, even when slowed by less-agile cubs. Daisy and her cubs migrated 40 air miles down the eastern side of the Continental Divide, eventually settling in the heart of the Sun River Game Range. They have not approached human settlements since then. The episode was a loss for the Missions, but a productive female survived to bolster the future of a threatened species.

In the moment when a great bear bounds from the cage that has briefly contained her, in the spine-tingling seconds she spends summoning her cubs and surveying her domain for a glimpse of her captors, there is an exhilaration that conveys both the darkest fears and the boundless joys that are the essence of the wilderness spirit. For the Salish and Kootenai people, still near in time to their wilderness roots, the Missions are a link with a heritage fast disappearing amid the frenzied press of civilization and change. For western culture, wilderness has become a place to rediscover the spirit of wildness and the richness and genetic diversity of the untamed world. The Missions are a meeting ground for both cultures, a place for them to rediscover their mutual roots in the unfettered earth that has shaped their destinies.

Montana Wilderness Areas

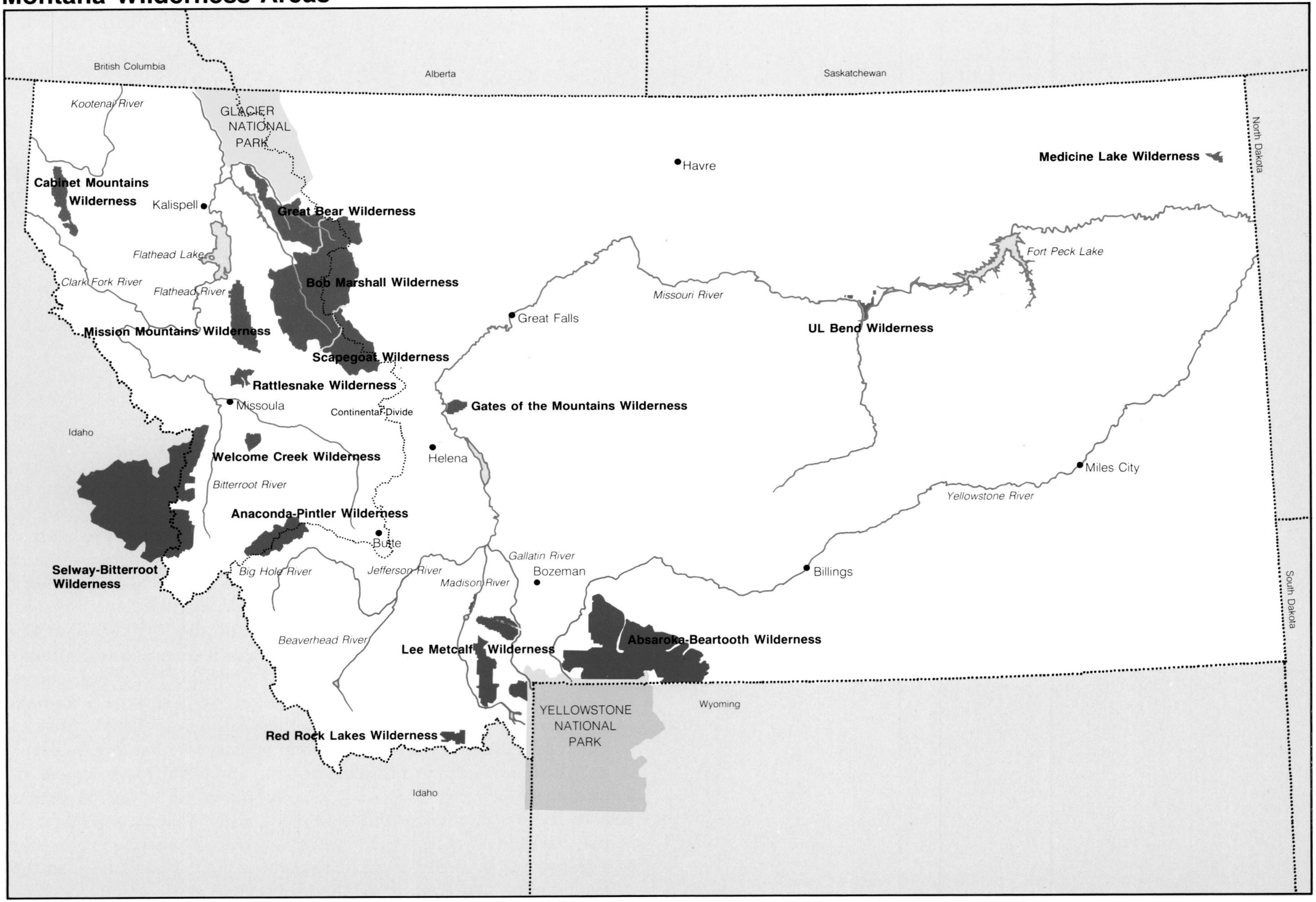

British Columbia

Alberta

Saskatchewan

Kootenai River

GLACIER
NATIONAL
PARK

●Havre

Medicine Lake Wilderness

North Dakota

**Cabinet Mountains
Wilderness**

Kalispell ●

Great Bear Wilderness

Flathead Lake

Fort Peck Lake

Clark Fork River

Bob Marshall Wilderness

Flathead River

Mission Mountains Wilderness

Missouri River

UL Bend Wilderness

Scapegoat Wilderness

Great Falls ●

Rattlesnake Wilderness

● Missoula

Continental Divide

Gates of the Mountains Wilderness

Idaho

Welcome Creek Wilderness

● Helena

● Miles City

Bitterroot River

Yellowstone River

Anaconda-Pintler Wilderness

● Butte

Gallatin River

**Selway-Bitterroot
Wilderness**

Big Hole River

Jefferson River

Bozeman ●

● Billings

Madison River

Absaroka-Beartooth Wilderness

Beaverhead River

Lee Metcalf Wilderness

YELLOWSTONE
NATIONAL
PARK

Wyoming

South Dakota

Red Rock Lakes Wilderness

Idaho

Chapter 12

EXPLORING THE WILDS

The best way to gain an understanding and appreciation of wilderness is to experience it firsthand

No PROSE, POETRY, or photograph can completely capture the magic and majesty of wilderness. The vastness of the land must be measured in a person's own paces. The beauty of a delicate alpine flower is something to see with one's own eyes, and the quiet moods inspired by the lonesome prairie can be felt only within one's own heart.

Books are one way of learning about the wilds. But the only way to know the wilderness is to experience it firsthand. Whether it is an expedition atop pinnacles of rock and ice or a short walk from the car for an afternoon's picnic, exploration is the key to understanding and appreciating wildland resources.

This chapter details 32 wilderness trips, each one highlighting specific features or issues discussed in previous chapters. The trip information is intended to be a starting point for wilderness travel and is not a tour guide. Information about each trip is limited largely to how to find the trailhead and where to go from there. What to see and do along the way, where to fish and hunt, and how best to enjoy the trip are matters of personal discovery. In some cases, campsite recommendations are included to steer people away from overused areas.

Some of the trips are quite difficult, requiring considerable experience, equipment, and stamina. Other trips are relatively easy and suitable for families or first-time wilderness adventurers. Additional information—available from maps and the agencies that manage the areas—might be necessary to plan a trip properly.

Montana's weather is extremely variable, especially in the mountainous portions of the state's western half. Even on short day trips, hikers should be prepared for dramatic changes in weather. Rain gear,

From the mountains to the prairies, the Big Sky Country, facing page, contains some of the most diverse wild land in the lower 48 states. By exploring the areas for themselves, people can gain a better understanding and appreciation of the wilderness.

warm clothing, emergency food, and fire-starting materials are a good idea for any trip. Maps and a compass, as well as the ability to use them, can improve the margin of safety in the backcountry.

Water quality can be a matter of concern even in the middle of the wilderness. Seemingly pure lakes and streams sometimes contain *Giardia lamblia,* a tiny parasite that can cause severe intestinal problems. Cautious hikers boil their water before drinking or cooking with it.

Much of Montana's wilderness is bear country. Problems with black and grizzly bears are rare, but a few incidents occur each year. Simple precautions, such as keeping a clean camp away from obvious bear sign, cooking away from sleeping areas, avoiding smelly foods, and suspending food and cooking utensils between tall trees away from camp, can reduce the chances of bear encounters.

Wilderness visitors can take other simple steps to protect the quality of the areas they visit. As a general rule, keep camps 200 feet from lakes and 150 feet from streams. In addition to preventing water pollution, keeping camps away from water will spare the most abused and overused campsites, which are usually situated along lakeshores. Leave the hatchets and saws at home, and use a small camp stove instead of a fire for cooking. If a fire is necessary, dig a shallow hole by removing and saving a chunk of sod or topsoil, and build the fire in the hole. Use only small, dead wood as fuel, and replace the sod or soil in the hole after making sure the fire is completely out. Bury human waste, but pack out all trash and garbage. Restore campsites as closely as possible to their natural conditions before leaving.

Any wilderness visit represents a challenge. Most trips require travel on foot, horseback, or canoe; successful orienteering and comfortable camping take a measure of woodsmanship skills. But the ultimate wilderness challenge is to visit the area without harming the special qualities that make it wild.

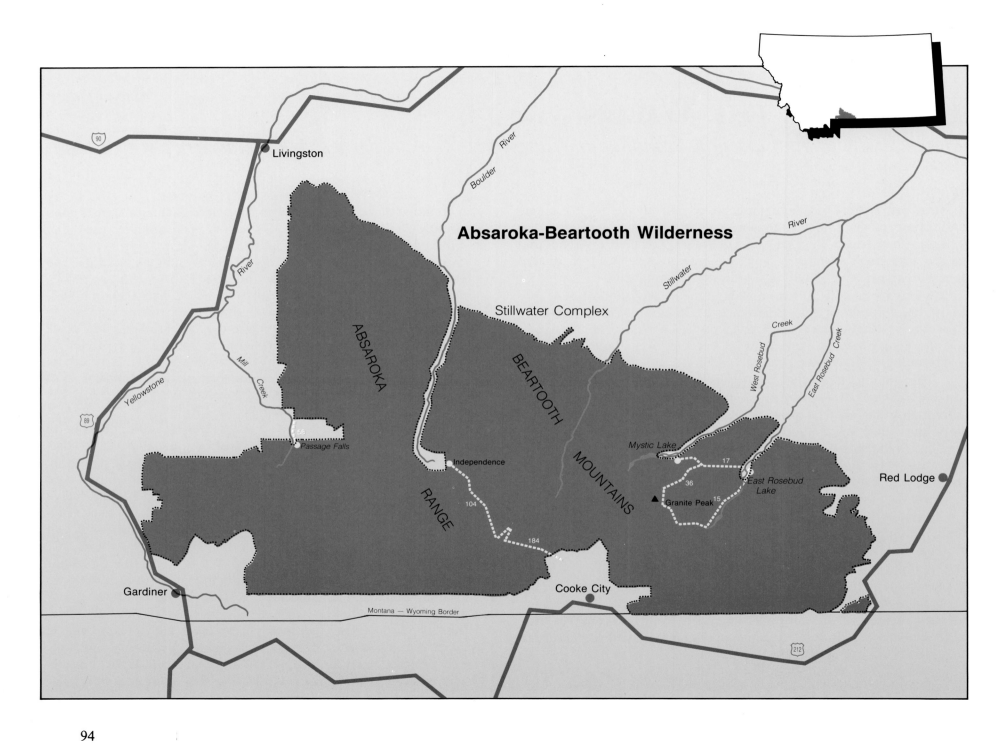

Absaroka-Beartooth Wilderness

Livingston

Boulder River

River

River

Stillwater River

Mill Creek

ABSAROKA

Stillwater Complex

Stillwater Creek

BEARTOOTH

West Rosebud Creek

East Rosebud Creek

Yellowstone

56

Passage Falls

MOUNTAINS

Mystic Lake

17

Independence

RANGE

36

East Rosebud Lake

Red Lodge

104

Granite Peak

15

184

Gardiner

Cooke City

Montana — Wyoming Border

212

ABSAROKA-BEARTOOTH

Alpine-to-Granite Peak

Round trip: about 30 miles. Hiking time: 3-5 days. Elevation gain: 6,326 feet to Mount Tempest. High point: 12,478 feet, Mount Tempest; 12,799 feet, Granite Peak. Best time: late July through early September. USGS maps: Alpine, Cooke City.

A tough expedition into some of the roughest and highest country Montana has to offer. From Highway 212 near Red Lodge, take Road 307 to Roscoe and Alpine. Trail 17 begins just north of the outlet to East Rosebud Lake. Beginning at an elevation of 6,133 feet, the trail climbs steeply past Slough Lake to the 10,000-foot-high Froze-to-Death Plateau. An alternate route beginning near Mystic Lake is shorter but even steeper. The two trails join on top of the plateau. Rock cairns mark Trail 36, which heads southwest from the trail junction, skirting Froze-to-Death Mountain on the way to Mount Tempest. Campsites are at a premium on the rocky plateau. Pick a spot that offers shelter from lightning and the wind, which often blows with enough intensity to collapse or shred all but the best tents. Firewood is nonexistent on the plateaus, and water must be captured from melting snowbanks. The saddle below Mount Tempest is a traditional base camp for climbing Granite Peak. Obtain a route description from the Red Lodge Ranger District of the Custer National Forest before scaling the peak. A difficult cross-country return route to Alpine begins in the saddle between Mount Tempest and Granite Peak, dropping steeply to Granite Lakes at the head of Granite Creek drainage. From the upper lake, descend the southwestern side of the drainage to Echo Lake, a trip of about 4 miles, depending on the route. The drainage alternates between boulders and perennial snowfields. Use of an ice axe is advisable along much of the way during the early summer. Crossing snowmelt-swollen Granite Creek, just above Echo Lake, requires extreme caution. A fisherman's trail connects Echo Lake with Trail 15, which leads northward past Lake at the Falls and Big Park, Rainbow, Rimrock, and Elk lakes on its way to Alpine.

Cooke City to Independence

One-way trip: 20 miles. Hiking time: 2-3 days. Elevation gain: 1,200 feet. High point: 9,631 feet. Best time: July through September. USGS maps: Cooke City, Cutoff Mountain, Mount Douglas.

A moderately difficult hike crossing from the Beartooths into the Absaroka Range. Environmentalists fought hard to persuade Congress to make the area the vital connecting link between the Absaroka and Beartooth portions of the wilderness. A one-way trip across the area requires two cars. Leave one vehicle at the end of the Boulder River Road, which is reached via Highway 298 from Big Timber. Begin the trip on Trail 184, just north of Cooke City. The route leads past Lake Abundance, following Abundance Creek. Near the halfway point, Trail 184 connects with Trail 104, which leads to Independence.

Passage Falls

Round trip: 5 miles. Hiking time: 3-6 hours. Elevation gain: 300 feet. High point: 6,500 feet. Best time: late May through September. USGS maps: Emigrant, Mount Wallace.

An easy hike to a beautiful waterfall on Passage Creek, which has been the subject of a lengthy controversy. From Highway 89 just north of Pray, take the Mill Creek Road to Trail 58. The trail follows stream grade through a timbered canyon, crossing several small meadows before reaching the falls a short distance inside the wilderness boundary. Passage Falls is at the northeastern corner of a picturesque old homestead located within view of Mount Wallace. Congress adjusted the wilderness boundary in 1983 to allow construction of a short road to the private property.

For additional information, contact Custer National Forest, P.O. Box 2556, Billings, MT 59103, (406) 657-6361; Gallatin National Forest, P.O. Box 130, Bozeman, MT 59715, (406) 587-5271.

SELWAY-BITTERROOT

Paradise to Darby

One-way trip: about 40 miles. Hiking time: 4-5 days. Elevation gain: 5,000 feet. High point: 8,160 feet. Best time: July through September. USGS maps: Burnt Strip Mountain, Watchtower Peak, Mount Paloma, Tin Cup Lake, Trapper Peak.

A long trek across the southern end of the wilderness, crossing from Idaho into Montana. Leave a car at the head of Tin Cup Trail 96 west of Darby. Take a second car south on Highway 93 to the West Fork Road,

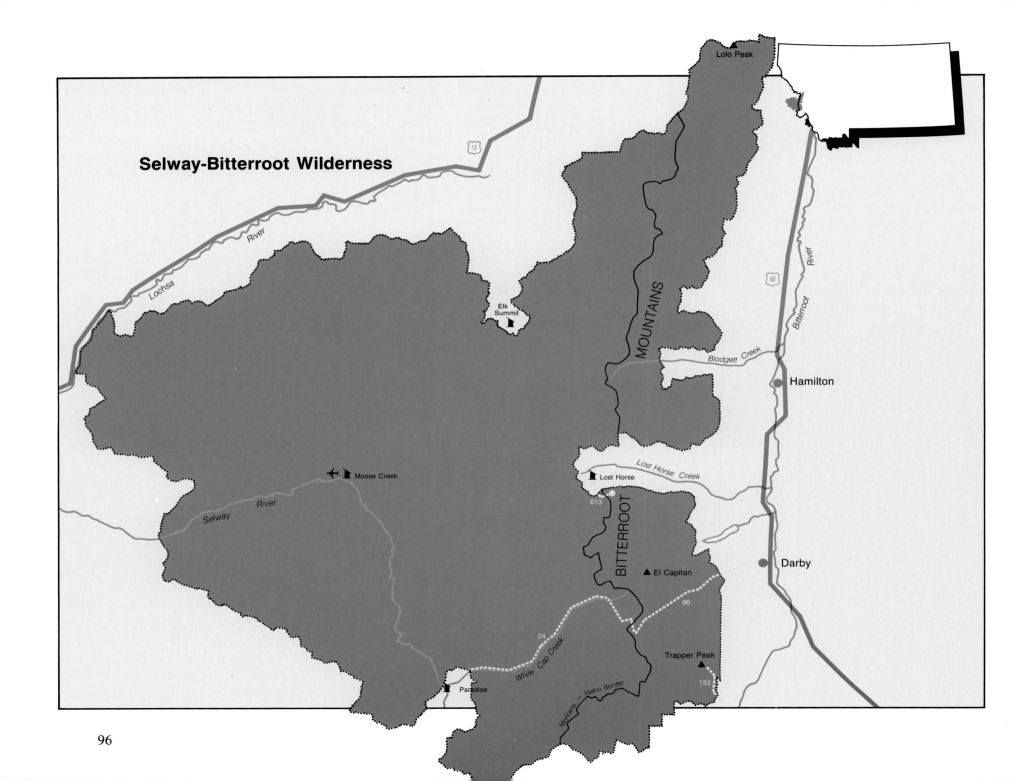

Selway-Bitterroot Wilderness

Lolo Peak

12

Lochsa River

Elk Summit

MOUNTAINS

93

Bitterroot River

Blodgett Creek

Hamilton

Moose Creek

Lost Horse Creek

Lost Horse

613

Selway River

BITTERROOT

El Capitan

Darby

96

24

White Cap Creek

Trapper Peak

Paradise

Montana — Idaho Border

133

96

crossing Nez Perce Pass into Idaho. The trailhead is at the end of Forest Service Road 6223. Trail 24 follows White Cap Creek and offers good views of areas burned by recent forest fires. It is a long 2.5-day hike to the Montana border at the crest of the Bitterroot Range. From Patsy Ann Falls, the trail becomes a series of steep switchbacks connecting with Trail 96 at the top of the divide. Another series of switchbacks descends to Tin Cup Lake, which is a day's hike from Darby. Cooper's Flat, Patsy Ann Falls, Triple Lakes, and Tin Cup Lake offer possible campsites along the route.

Lolo Peak

Round trip: 12 miles. Hiking time: 1 day. Elevation gain: 3,296 feet. High point: 9,096 feet. Best time: June through September. USGS map: Carlton Lake.

A steep, but otherwise easy climb to the top of a well-known western Montana landmark, with views of mountains and surrounding valleys in two states. From Highway 12 west of Lolo, turn left on the Mormon Creek Road. Trail 1311 begins at the last hairpin turn before the old Mormon Peak lookout. The trail starts out gently, then climbs straight up a steep timbered ridge overlooking Carlton Lake, which is on the northern boundary of the wilderness. The trail to the summit circles the eastern end of the lake. An unmarked route around the western shore is shorter but requires a scramble to the ridge leading to the peak.

Fish Lake

Round trip: 7 miles. Hiking time: 1-2 days. Elevation gain: 960 feet. High point: 7,160 feet. Best time: late June through September. USGS map: El Capitan.

An easy overnight trip to a sparkling lake beneath the crest of the Bitterroot Range. From Highway 93 south of Hamilton, take the Lost Horse Road to Bear Creek Pass, located just west of the Idaho State Line. Trail 613 follows an easy, but muddy route past Lower Bear Lake before turning east. A short series of switchbacks leads over a low divide, dropping to Fish Lake on the Montana side of the wilderness. Hackney, Coquina, and Lower Bear lakes are within easy day-trip distance of Fish Lake.

Trapper Peak

Round trip: 10 miles. Hiking time: 1 day. Elevation gain: 3,755 feet.

High point: 10,157 feet. Best time: May through September. USGS maps: Boulder Peak, Trapper Peak.

A long uphill hike to the highest peak in the wilderness, offering views of the Bitterroot Range and nearby valleys. From Highway 93 south of Darby, take the West Fork Road to Forest Service Road 5630A. Trail 133 climbs steeply from the trailhead to the wilderness boundary at the top of the ridge. The trail follows the ridge to timberline at 9,000 feet, then climbs just south of the ridge edge to the summit. Beware of snow cornices on the northern edge of the ridge during the spring and early summer.

For additional information, contact the Bitterroot National Forest, 316 N. Third St., Hamilton, MT 59840, (406) 363-3131; Lolo National Forest, Building 24, Fort Missoula, Missoula, MT 59801, (406) 329-3557; Clearwater National Forest, 12730 Highway 12, Orofino, Idaho 83544, (208) 476-4541; Nezperce National Forest, Route 2, Box 475, Grangeville, Idaho 83530, (208) 983-1950.

LEE METCALF

Beartrap Canyon

One-way trip: 9 miles. Travel time: 4-6 hours. Elevation drop: 200 feet. High point: 4,800 feet. Best time: late May through September. USGS maps: Ennis, Norris.

A relatively easy hike or a challenging white-water raft trip through a deep, rugged canyon. To reach the upstream end of the canyon, take Highway 287 to McAllister. Drive east on the dirt road to the powerhouse below Ennis Lake. The Montana Power Company, which owns the road below the lake, allows access to rafters. Parking space is extremely limited. The upstream end of the canyon is closed to hiking access because the trail passes through the dangerous overflow chute for the powerhouse. Hikers must enter from the Beartrap Recreation Area between Norris and Bozeman. The Madison River has several major rapids in Beartrap Canyon, the largest of which is the Kitchen Sink. The river may be dangerous or impassable for inexperienced rafters when the water flows exceed 3,000 cubic feet per second. At least one commercial outfitter offers float trips through Beartrap. A narrow hiking trail follows the eastern side of the river. Rattlesnakes are especially plentiful in the rocky canyon.

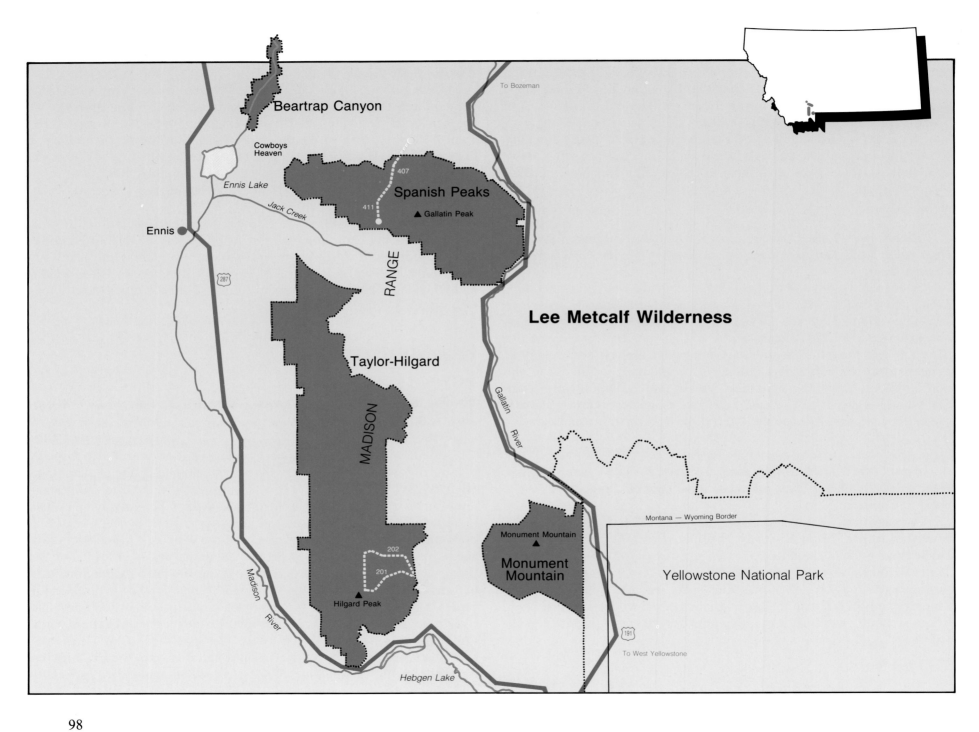

Beartrap Canyon

Cowboys
Heaven

Ennis Lake

Jack Creek

407

Spanish Peaks

411

▲ Gallatin Peak

Ennis

RANGE

287

Taylor-Hilgard

Lee Metcalf Wilderness

Gallatin River

MADISON

Madison River

202

201

Montana — Wyoming Border

▲ Monument Mountain

Monument
Mountain

Yellowstone National Park

▲ Hilgard Peak

191

To Bozeman

To West Yellowstone

Hebgen Lake

Spanish Lakes

Round trip: 16 miles. Hiking time: 2-3 days. Elevation gain: 2,800 feet. High point: 6,800 feet. Best time: July through September. USGS map: Spanish Peaks.

A moderate hike through a lodgepole pine forest to a cluster of small alpine lakes beneath 10,000-foot-high peaks. The trailhead is at Spanish Creek Guard Station, a 9-mile drive from Highway 191 south of Bozeman. Trail 407 parallels the western side of the South Fork of Spanish Creek roughly 4 miles before turning onto Trail 411. The route has a fairly easy grade, but the last mile to the lakes climbs steeply. The Spanish Lakes are a popular destination, making no-trace camping practices essential to maintaining their wilderness qualities. From the lakes, it is a relatively easy climb to the top of the unnamed peaks to the south, which offer a spectacular view of the Madison Range.

Hilgard Basin

Round trip: 14 miles. Hiking time: 2-3 days. Elevation gain: 2,400 feet. High point: 9,600 feet. Best time: late July through September. USGS map: Hebgen Dam.

A fairly easy hike into the heart of the Taylor-Hilgard portion of the Lee Metcalf Wilderness. Trail 202 is located at the end of Beaver Creek Road, north of Highway 287 near Earthquake Lake. The trail begins at Polomageton Park, climbing an average of about 400 feet a mile to Expedition Lake at the northern end of the basin. More than a dozen alpine lakes are scattered through the basin, all within view of spectacular high peaks. For a loop trip back to the trailhead, travel south through the basin, returning on Trail 201.

For additional information, contact the Beaverhead National Forest, P.O. Box 1258, Dillon, MT 59725, (406) 683-2312; Gallatin National Forest, P.O. Box 130, Bozeman, MT 59715, (406) 587-5271; Bureau of Land Management, P.O. Box 3388, Butte, MT 59702, (406) 494-5059.

BOB MARSHALL

Headquarters Pass to Gates Park

Round trip: 30 miles. Hiking time: 2-3 days. Elevation gain: 2,534 feet.

High point: 7,743 feet. Best time: July through September. USGS maps: Gates Park, Our Lake.

A moderate trip that enters the wilderness just north of its highest peak, then drops down to a backcountry guard station located on the North Fork of the Sun River in a series of meadows that were once homesteaded. From U.S. 89, turn west on county road 144 about 5 miles north of Choteau. Drive about 15 miles, turn south, and cross the river, following county road 109 up the South Fork of the Teton River to the road's end. Trail 165 follows the South Fork about 6 miles to Headquarters Pass, with a couple of steep switchback climbs near the upper end. This is mountain goat and sheep country. Camp a mile or two beyond the pass, in the upper Headquarters Creek basins. From here the trail drops 8 miles down the creek to the guard station, crossing the North Fork of the Sun River on a pack bridge. Camp away from the overused sites along the river.

Benchmark-Holland Lake

One-way trip: 60 miles. Hiking time: 6-8 days. Elevation gain: 2,130 feet, Benchmark to White River Pass; 3,280 feet, South Fork to Swan Range crest. High point: 7,660 feet. Best time: July through October. USGS maps: Benchmark, Pretty Prairie, Prairie Reef, Haystack Mountain, Big Salmon Lake East, Pagoda Mountain, Big Salmon Lake West, Holland Peak, Holland Lake.

A week-long trip through the heart of the Bob Marshall, following a network of national forest trails. Use two vehicles. Park one at Holland Campground on Holland Lake, 18 miles north of Seeley Lake on Montana Highway 83. Then make the 130-mile drive south on Montana 83, east on Montana 200, and north on U.S. 287 to Augusta. Take Forest Service Road 235 from the southern edge of Augusta, and head northwest 30 miles to the road's end at Benchmark. Take Trail 202, a gentle, but heavily used route, north along the South Fork of the Sun River for 5 miles, crossing the river's West Fork on a pack bridge. Continue 8 miles on Trail 203 past the Indian Point Guard Station. A 4-mile side trip on Trail 224 to Prairie Reef Lookout, 1.5 miles before Indian Point, offers a fine view of the Chinese Wall. Ford the West Fork about 1 mile past Indian Point, and follow Trail 211 along Indian Creek about 6 miles to White River Pass near the southern end of the Chinese Wall. Camp off the trail in the timber east of the pass. The pass is a starting place for a cross-country exploration of the wall. Water can be

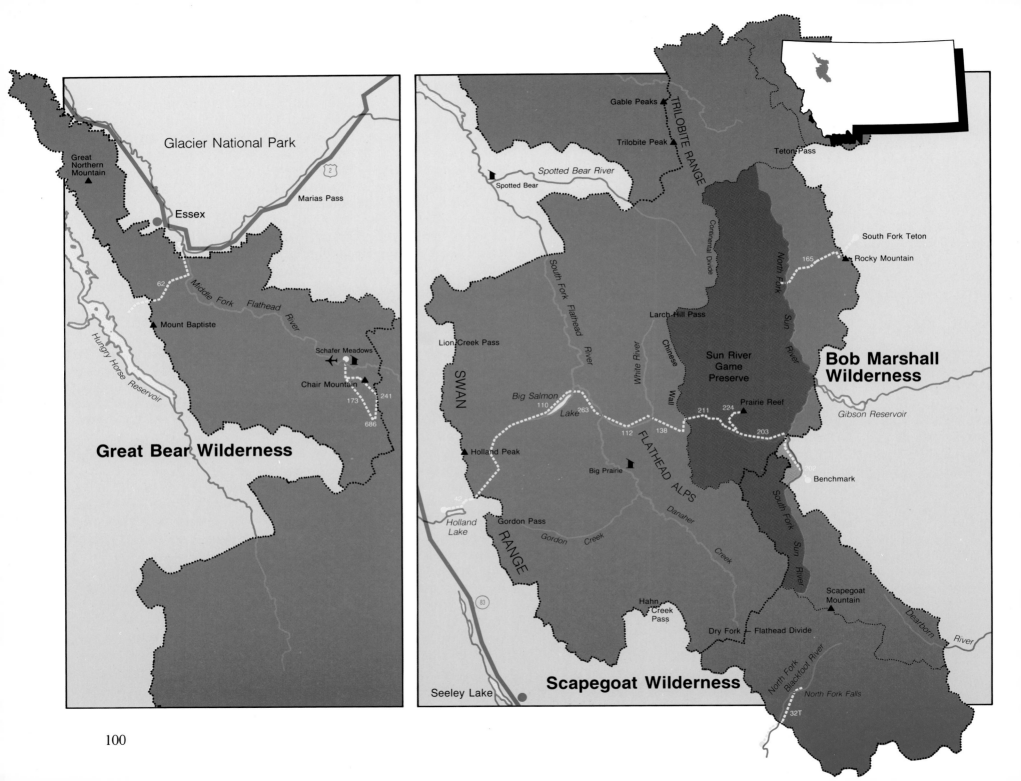

Glacier National Park

Great Northern Mountain

Essex

Marias Pass

62

Middle Fork Flathead River

Mount Baptiste

Schafer Meadows

Chair Mountain

173 241

686

Hungry Horse Reservoir

Great Bear Wilderness

Gable Peaks

TRILOBITE RANGE

Trilobite Peak

Teton Pass

Spotted Bear River

Spotted Bear

South Fork Teton

165

Rocky Mountain

Continental Divide

Larch Hill Pass

North Fork Sun River

South Fork Flathead River

White River

Chinese Wall

Sun River Game Preserve

Bob Marshall Wilderness

Lion Creek Pass

SWAN

Big Salmon Lake

110 263

112

138

211 224

Prairie Reef

203

Gibson Reservoir

Holland Peak

Big Prairie

FLATHEAD ALPS

202

Benchmark

42

Holland Lake

Gordon Pass

Gordon Creek

Danaher Creek

South Fork Sun River

RANGE

83

Hahn Creek Pass

Scapegoat Mountain

Dry Fork — Flathead Divide

Dearborn River

Seeley Lake

Scapegoat Wilderness

North Fork Blackfoot River

North Fork Falls

32T

100

scarce at the pass. The trail drops quickly from the pass, with a good view of the Flathead Alps to the southwest. In 5 miles, the trail joins the White River. A side trip 3 miles up the White River reaches Needle Falls. The main trail continues 6 miles west along the northern bank of the White River to the big parks along the South Fork. Camp at White River Park, or ford the river to Murphy Flat. Heed the Forest Service signs directing campers away from campsite restoration areas. From there, head downstream 5 miles to Salmon Forks, and turn west to Big Salmon Lake. The trail follows the northern shore of the lake for about 6 miles. Continue west and south along Big Salmon Creek about 10 miles to Big Salmon Falls. Then bear west up Smoky Creek another 2 miles toward the Necklace Lakes. The last leg crosses the top of the Swan Range.

GREAT BEAR
Schafer Meadow to Gable Peaks and Chair Mountain

Round trip: 17 miles. Hiking time: 2 days. Elevation gain: 2,145 feet. High point: 7,000 feet. Best time: late July through September. USGS maps: Gable Peaks, Trilobite Peak.

A loop hike requiring a flight to Schafer Airstrip. The flight costs $82 to $90 each way for three people. The wilderness is a magnificent sight from the air, and the flight provides quick access to remote country. The hike from Schafer is over a lightly used trail. From Schafer Ranger Station, follow Trail 327 east and south, fording the Middle Fork of the Flathead River and branching southeast within a mile on Trail 173 along Dolly Varden Creek. The trail climbs gently through lodgepole, passing the Chair Mountain Trail 241 after the second mile. Continue another 6 miles to Trail 686. Campsites are available near the trail junction. Climb up Trail 686, which later rejoins Trail 241. The trail wends through old burns and along the limestone escarpments of the northern Trilobite Range, then drops down Chair Mountain in a series of steep switchbacks. For a longer trip, spend an extra day exploring the high ridges and climbing Trilobite or Gable Peaks.

Logan Creek-Dirtyface Creek

Round trip: 14 miles. Hiking time: 2 days. Elevation gain: 2,300 feet. High point: 6,300 feet. Best time: July through September. USGS maps: Felix Peak, Nimrod.

An overnight hike across the Flathead Range and the northern panhandle of the wilderness, featuring mountain meadows and a scenic waterfall. From U.S. 2 at Martin City, follow Forest Service Road 38 south along the eastern side of Hungry Horse Reservoir. Then turn east at Logan Creek on Forest Service Road 1632, and drive 2 miles to the trailhead. Trail 62 follows Logan Creek to the Flathead divide. Camp at the top. Continue 7 miles east down Dirtyface Creek to the Middle Fork of the Flathead River. Ford the river, and go north 2.5 miles on Big River Trail 55 to U.S. 2 at Bear Creek.

SCAPEGOAT
North Fork Falls

Round trip: 14 miles. Hiking time: 2 days. Elevation gain: 660 feet. High point: 5,450 feet. Best time: June through September. USGS maps: Coopers Lake, Lake Mountain.

A long day hike or short overnight trip to a major wilderness falls on the North Fork of the Blackfoot River. From Montana 200, turn north on Forest Service Road 500 about 17 miles west of Lincoln. Follow the road 12 miles north to the trailhead. Trail 32 follows the North Fork canyon, climbing gently but steadily. Wooden bridges cross the river twice. The North Fork Guard Station, a wilderness ranger station, is in a pleasant clearing about 6.5 miles from the trailhead. One-half mile farther, the river thunders in two cascades through a deep, narrow gorge carved in colorful rock. The lower falls drops 100 feet or more. Camp above the falls or near the guard station, and return by the same route.

For additional information about the Bob Marshall Complex, contact the Flathead National Forest, P.O. Box 147, Kalispell, MT 59901, (406) 755-5401; Lewis and Clark National Forest, Box 871, Great Falls, MT 59923, (406) 293-6211; Helena National Forest, Drawer 10014, Helena, MT 59626, (406) 449-5201; Lolo National Forest, Building 24, Fort Missoula, Missoula, MT 59801, (406) 329-3557.

ANACONDA-PINTLER
Phyllis Lakes

Round trip: 10 miles. Hiking time: 2 days. Elevation gain: 1,800 feet.

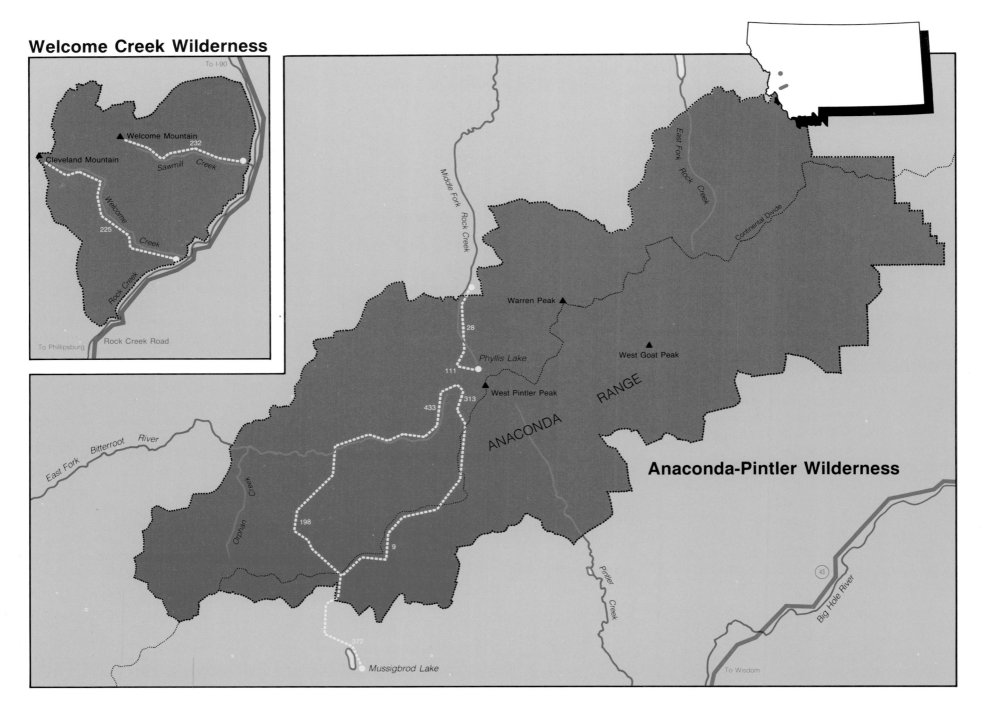

Welcome Creek Wilderness

To I-90

Welcome Mountain

232

Cleveland Mountain

Sawmill Creek

Welcome

225

Creek

Rock Creek

To Phillipsburg

Rock Creek Road

Middle Fork Rock Creek

East Fork Rock Creek

Continental Divide

Warren Peak

28

West Goat Peak

Phyllis Lake

111

West Pintler Peak

RANGE

313

433

ANACONDA

Anaconda-Pintler Wilderness

East Fork Bitterroot River

Orphan Creek

198

9

Pintler Creek

43

Big Hole River

372

Mussigbrod Lake

To Wisdom

High point: 8,160 feet. Best time: late July through early September. USGS map: Kelly Lake.

A moderately strenuous hike on a good trail that climbs to a pair of lakes below West Pintler Peak in the heart of the wilderness. From Highway 10-A north of Georgetown Lake, head west on Montana 38. Then turn south on Forest Service Road 5106. Follow the Middle Fork of Rock Creek about 20 miles past Moose Lake to the trailhead. Take Trail 28 about 4 miles, and bear east on Trail 111 at the junction by the meadow. Ambitious hikers can set up a base camp, scramble up West Pintler, and drop down into several nearby lakes. The shores of Upper Phyllis Lake are heavily marred by camping, but a skilled camper can move off into the lodgepole east of the lake and camp in privacy without leaving a trace.

Continental Divide

Round trip: 40 miles. Hiking time: 5 days. Elevation gain: 2,040 feet. High point: 8,600 feet. Best time: August. USGS maps: Mussigbrod Lake, Bender Point, Kelly Lake.

An extended loop trip for experienced overnight campers, offering a 10-mile ridge walk on the Continental Divide. To reach the trailhead, turn north off Montana 43 about 1 mile west of Wisdom, and follow the county road about 20 miles west to Mussigbrod Lake. From Mussigbrod Campground, follow Trail 372 around the lake. About 1 mile past the lake, the trail bears north up Mussigbrod Creek at the junction with Trail 379. It switchbacks through a lodgepole forest to a long ridge that leads up to the Divide. Turn east on Trail 9 at the four-way junction on top. This section of the Divide trail is fairly heavily used. Continue about 1.5 miles to the junction with Trail 424 in the saddle above Hope Lake. The lake is about one-half mile away and 500 feet down. Campsites are limited, and the trail down is closed to horses and stock. The Divide trail continues northeast, climbing up and down along the ridges, crossing the high basins above Alpine Lakes, Mystic Lake, and Park Lakes. Plimpton Creek Trail 371 joins from the south about one-half mile past the Hope Lake trail junction. Mystic Lake Trail 7 joins after 4 miles. Leave Trail 9 after about 8 miles, and follow Trail 313 northwest down into the headwaters of the East Fork of the Bitterroot River. Camp in the headwater basins a mile or two below the junction, or make a 1-mile side trip up Trail 401 to Hidden Lake. Avoid camping on the lakeshore, which gets a lot of use. Follow Trail 313, but bear south down Trail 433

about one-half mile past the Hidden Lake trail junction. For a side trip to Kelly Lake, stay on 313 another mile, and note where Trail 402 branches south to Ripple Lake on the last low ridge before Kelly. Continue down Trail 433, following the East Fork about 5 miles to Star Falls, an impressive 60-foot cascade. Buck Creek Trail 198 is 2 miles farther at Kurtz Flats. Camp near the trail junction. Follow Trail 198 across the East Fork and up Buck Creek, climbing steadily for 2,600 feet and crossing Buck Creek twice. Camp at Buck Ridge Meadows, just below the Divide. Continue to the Divide on Trail 198, and head down Trail 372, retracing the first day's route to the trailhead.

For additional information, contact the Beaverhead National Forest, P.O. Box 1258, Dillon, MT 59725, (406) 683-2312; Deerlodge National Forest, P.O. Box 400, Butte, MT 59703, (406) 723-6561; Bitterroot National Forest, 316 N. Third St., Hamilton, MT 59840, (406) 363-3131.

WELCOME CREEK

Welcome Creek to Cleveland Mountain

Round trip: 20 miles. Hiking time: 2 days. Elevation gain: 3,200 feet. High point: 7,240 feet. Best time: July through October. USGS maps: Cleveland Mountain, Ravenna.

An overnight hike along the central artery of the wilderness to the top of the Sapphire divide. The trail follows Welcome Creek to its headwaters, through steep timbered canyons and past old mining cabins and digs. From the Rock Creek exit on Interstate 90 east of Missoula, drive south about 15 miles to the Welcome Creek Wilderness entrance. Cross the suspension footbridge over Rock Creek, and follow Trail 225 to the top. Camp in the lodgepole forests near the top or at Spartan Creek, about 7 miles up, and finish the ascent in the morning before the return trip down.

Sawmill Creek to Welcome Mountain

Round trip: 18 miles. Hiking time: 2 days. Elevation gain: 3,879 feet. High point: 7,723 feet. Best time: July through October. USGS maps: Cleveland Mountain, Ravenna.

A demanding overnight hike to the top of the highest mountain in the wilderness. Start from the Sawmill fishing access point at about mile

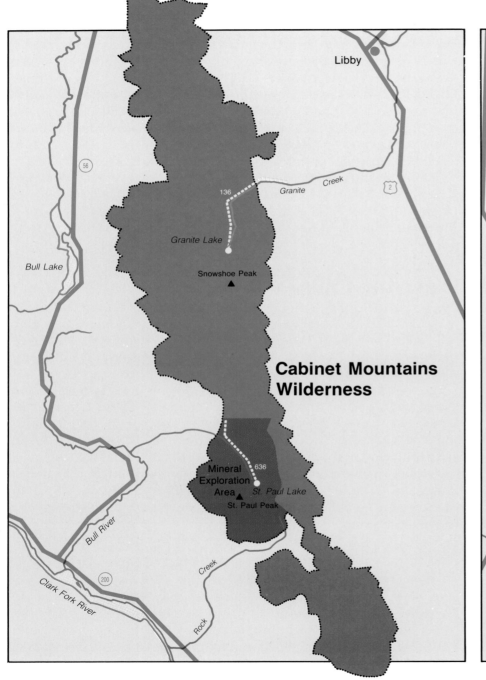

Cabinet Mountains Wilderness

Libby

56

136

Granite Creek

2

Granite Lake

Snowshoe Peak

Bull Lake

Mineral Exploration Area

636

St. Paul Lake

St. Paul Peak

Bull River

Creek

Rock

200

Clark Fork River

104

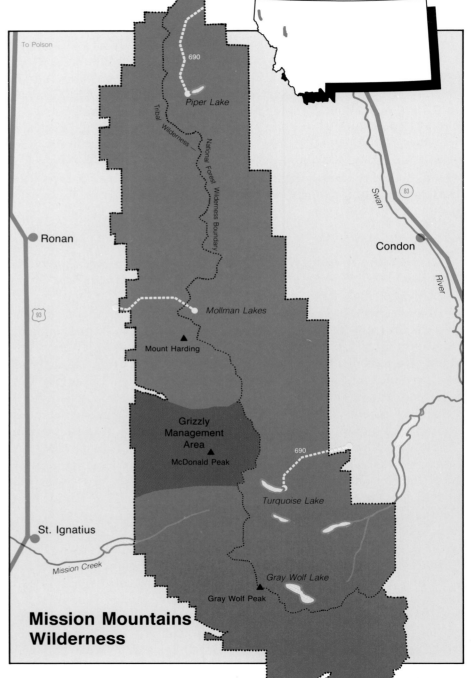

To Polson

690

Piper Lake

Tribal Wilderness

National Forest Wilderness Boundary

Ronan

93

Mollman Lakes

Mount Harding

Grizzly Management Area

McDonald Peak

690

Turquoise Lake

St. Ignatius

Mission Creek

Gray Wolf Lake

Gray Wolf Peak

Swan

83

Condon

River

Mission Mountains Wilderness

9 on the Rock Creek Road. Follow the creek west about three-quarters of a mile, and ford at the footings of an old cable crossing. Head up Sawmill Creek on Trail 178, which can be hard to find. The trail switchbacks up the hillside north of the creek to Solomon Ridge, Solomon Mountain, and Welcome Mountain. After about 6 miles, the trail crosses the old Welcome Mountain Road, which was built for logging the area but abandoned when Welcome Creek became a wilderness.

For additional information, contact the Lolo National Forest, Building 24, Fort Missoula, Missoula, MT 59801, (406) 329-3557.

Mission Mountains
Cedar Lake

Round trip: 8 miles. Hiking time: 2 days. Elevation gain: 1,100 feet. High point: 6,500 feet. Best time: July through October. USGS map: Cedar Lake.

An easy hike to an 80-acre lake in mostly alpine timber on the northern end of the Missions. Reach the trailhead from Highway 83 in the Swan Valley. Turn west one-quarter mile south of the Swan River Work Center, and follow the South Woodward Creek Road and Fatty Creek Road about 10 miles. A small campground is at the end of the road, where Trail 690 begins. The grassy summit of Cedar Peak, at 7,592 feet, is a fairly easy scramble from the lake. For a long day or overnight hike, continue past Cedar Lake another 3 miles to Piper Lake.

Mollman Lakes

Round trip: 8 miles. Hiking time: 2 days. Elevation gain: 3,300 feet. High point: 6,920 feet. Best time: mid-July through early October. USGS map: Mount Harding.

A very strenuous trip up the western face of the Missions to Mollman Pass and a cluster of two lakes and four potholes just east of the pass. Turn east from U.S. 93 toward the Kicking Horse Job Center about 3 miles south of Ronan. Follow a county road 4 miles to the trailhead. The hike offers magnificent vistas. This is tribal land, and a tribal recreation use permit is required for non-members.

Turquoise Lake

Round trip: 8 miles. Hiking time: 2 days. Elevation gain: 1,550 feet.

High point: 6,424 feet. Best time: mid-July through September. USGS maps: Hemlock, Grey Wolf Lake.

A moderately strenuous trip to a cluster of four lakes, of which the largest and most spectacular is Turquoise. From Montana 83, turn west about 5 miles north of the Clearwater-Swan Divide, and follow the Kraft Creek Road 561 about 12 miles to the trailhead. This long, deep, 200-acre lake fills a cliff-lined valley far below Glacier Peaks, Sunrise Glacier, and the Garden Wall of the Missions. A tumbling stream connects Turquoise with nearby Lace Lake.

For additional information, contact the Flathead National Forest, P.O. Box 147, Kalispell, MT 59901, (406) 755-5401; Confederated Salish and Kootenai Tribes, Department of Wildlands Recreation, Tribal Complex, P.O. Box 278, Pablo, MT 59855, (406) 675-4600.

Cabinet Mountains
St. Paul Lake

Round trip: 8 miles. Hiking time: 1 day. Elevation gain: 1,614 feet. High point: 4,715 feet. Best time: June through October. USGS map: Elephant Peak.

An easy hike into the southwestern Cabinets through cedar and spruce forests to a small lake nestled amid mountain peaks. Reach Trail 646 from Montana Highway 202 via Forest Service Road 407, which follows the East Fork of the Bull River. A good trail ascends gradually, with a short, steep climb for the last quarter mile. The hike features spectacular vistas of Bald Eagle, Elephant, Rock, and St. Paul peaks in the heart of the country where copper and silver mining claims have been staked.

Granite Lake

Round trip: 12 miles. Hiking time: 2 days. Elevation gain: 1,465 feet. High point: 4,605 feet. Best time: June through October. USGS maps: Treasure Mountain.

An easy hike into the central Cabinets to a deep, 40-acre lake nestled at the base of A Peak. The trail follows Granite Creek. Reach Trail 136 south of Libby on Forest Service Road 618.

For additional information, contact the Kootenai National Forest, P.O. Box AS, Libby, MT 59923, (406) 293-6211.

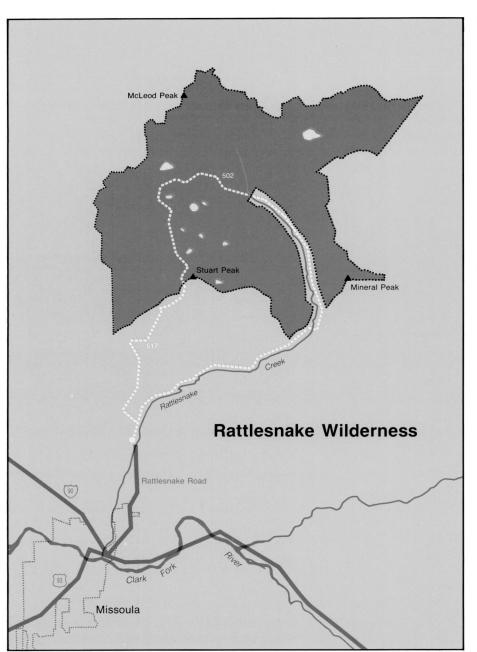

Rattlesnake Wilderness

McLeod Peak ▲

502

Stuart Peak ▲

Mineral Peak ▲

517

Creek

Rattlesnake

Rattlesnake Road

90

Clark Fork River

93

Missoula

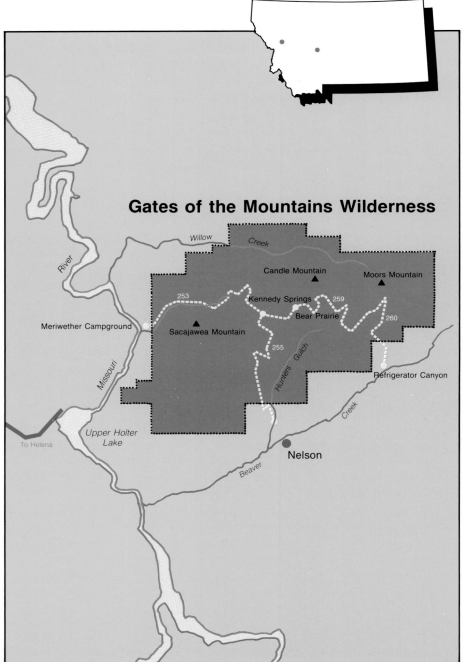

Gates of the Mountains Wilderness

River

Willow   Creek

Candle Mountain ▲

Moors Mountain ▲

253

Kennedy Springs   259

Bear Prairie

260

Meriwether Campground

Sacajawea Mountain ▲

255

Hunters Gulch

Refrigerator Canyon

Missouri

To Helena

Upper Holter Lake

Beaver   Creek

Nelson

GATES OF THE MOUNTAINS

Hunters Gulch to Refrigerator Canyon

Round trip: 18 miles. Hiking time: 2-3 days. Elevation gain: 2,300 feet. High point: 6,500 feet. Best time: late May or June. USGS maps: Candle Mountain, Nelson, Hogback Mountain.

A moderate trip through the southern half of the wilderness and proposed additions. From Helena, follow Montana 280 to York, and turn north on Forest Service Road 224 to Nelson and the Hunter's Gulch trailhead. Follow Trail 255 about 5 miles to the trail junction at Kennedy Springs. Turn east on Trail 253, which turns into Trail 259 within a mile when Trail 252 branches off down Willow Creek. Camp at Bear Prairie, about a mile past the Willow Creek trail junction. Continue east on Trail 259 past Candle Mountain and around Moors Mountain. In about 5 miles, as the trail descends the southern side of Moors Mountain, watch for the junction with Trail 260, and follow that trail south down to Refrigerator Canyon. The trail ends at Forest Service Road 138. Follow the road west about 5 miles back to Nelson and the starting point.

Refrigerator Canyon to Meriwether Campground

Round trip: 17 miles. Hiking time: 2 days. Elevation gain: 2,100 feet. High point: 6,500 feet. Best time: June. USGS maps: Candle Mountain, Nelson, Hogback Mountain, Upper Holter, Beartooth Mountain.

An overnight trip crossing the length of the wilderness, ending with a lovely boat trip down the Missouri River through the Gates of the Mountains. It is easiest with two vehicles, one parked at the end point. From Helena, take Interstate 15 north 16 miles to Gates of the Mountains Boat Club. Park one vehicle, and pick up the tour boat schedule. Then backtrack on the interstate, Montana 453, and Montana 280 to York. Turn north on Forest Service Road 224 to Nelson, and head east 4 miles on Forest Service Road 138 to the trailhead at Refrigerator Canyon. Follow Trail 260 north 3.5 miles, and head west up Trail 259 at the junction below Moors Mountain. Continue on Trail 259 about 5 miles to camp at Bear Prairie. On the second day, continue west on Trails 259 and 253 past Kennedy Springs and down Meriwether Canyon to Meriwether Campground. Catch the tour boat for the ride back to the boat club.

For additional information, contact the Helena National Forest, Drawer 10014, Helena, MT 59626, (406) 449-5201.

RATTLESNAKE

Stuart Peak-Rattlesnake Ridge

Round trip: 19 miles. Hiking time: 1-2 days. Elevation gain: 4,360 feet. High point: 7,960 feet. Best time: June through October. USGS maps: Northeast Missoula, Stuart Peak.

A long, steady climb for views of the Missoula Valley and surrounding mountains. Take Van Buren Street north from Missoula, and continue on Rattlesnake Road to Sawmill Gulch Road, the first left turn after Madera Street. The trailhead is located just west of the creek. The trail starts along the old Rattlesnake Road but turns to the northwest at Spring Gulch. The trail is easy at first, then becomes quite steep and filled with switchbacks after the first 3 miles. Water is scarce along the way. From Stuart Peak, much of the Rattlesnake Wilderness is within relatively easy reach via a well-maintained ridge-top trail. Numerous lakes are located along the eastern foot of the ridge. Watch for dangerous cornices of snow along the eastern side of the ridge in winter and early spring.

Rattlesnake Creek-Glacier Lake

Round trip: 35 miles. Hiking time: 2-4 days. Elevation gain: 3,400 feet. High point: 7,000 feet. Best time: June through October, January through February. USGS maps: Northeast Missoula, Stuart Peak, Blue Point, Wapiti Lake.

A long, but easy hiking, snowshoeing, or cross-country skiing trip along picturesque Rattlesnake Creek to a pair of beautiful lake basins. Much of the trail follows the old Rattlesnake Road through a non-wilderness corridor. After the first 5 miles, the wilderness boundary is scarcely 100 yards on each side of the trail. The route leads from the Missoula suburbs past abandoned homesteads and through the narrow, gently climbing Rattlesnake Valley. Rattlesnake Creek is within sight for most of the route, with many good spots for camping after the first 5 miles. At Mile 13, the trail forks toward the headwaters of Rattlesnake, Wrangle, and Lake creeks. Take Trail 502 about 3 miles to Little Lake, then another mile to Glacier Lake. Located beneath Mosquito Peak, both lakes offer good campsites. From Glacier Lake, it is a short, steep climb to the top of Rattlesnake Ridge.

For additional information, contact the Lolo National Forest, Building 24, Fort Missoula, Missoula, MT 59801, (406) 329-3557.

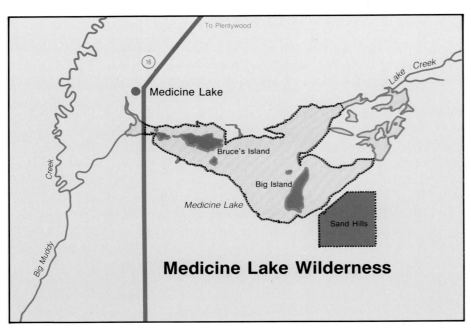

Medicine Lake Wilderness

Map labels: To Plentywood, 16, Medicine Lake, Lake Creek, Bruce's Island, Big Island, Medicine Lake, Sand Hills, Creek, Big Muddy

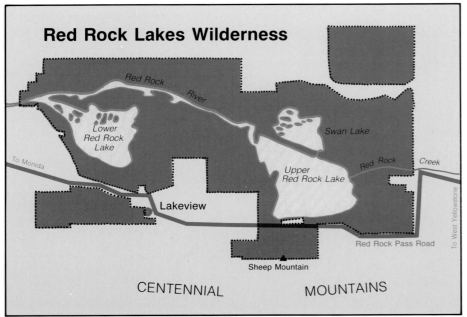

Red Rock Lakes Wilderness

Map labels: Red Rock River, Lower Red Rock Lake, Swan Lake, Upper Red Rock Lake, Red Rock Creek, To Monida, Lakeview, Red Rock Pass Road, To West Yellowstone, Sheep Mountain, CENTENNIAL MOUNTAINS

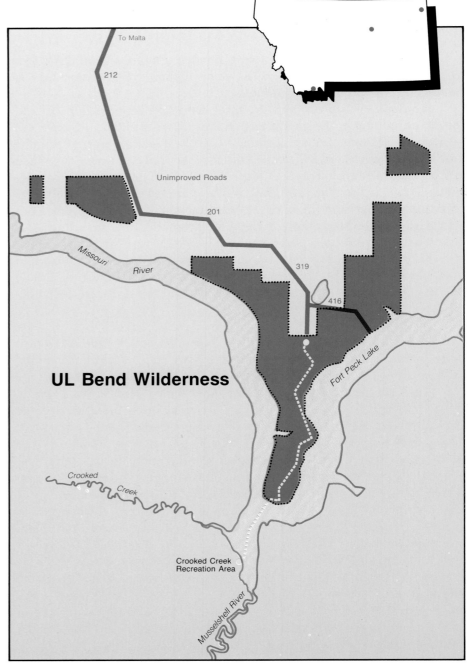

UL Bend Wilderness

Map labels: To Malta, 212, 201, 319, 416, Unimproved Roads, Missouri River, Fort Peck Lake, Crooked Creek, Crooked Creek Recreation Area, Musselshell River

RED ROCK LAKES

Upper Red Rock Lake

Round trip: 10 miles. Travel time: 6-8 hours. Best time: July 15 through October. USGS map: Upper Red Rock Lake.

A long day's canoe trip around the marshy shore of Upper Red Rock Lake with excellent opportunities for observing waterfowl and shorebirds. Access to the lake is from the campground on the southern shore. To reach the campground, take the Red Rock Pass road east from Lima or west from Henrys Lake, Idaho. Boats without motors are allowed on the lake only after July 15. Dense vegetation and marshy conditions make exploring the shoreline on foot difficult. Red Rock Creek, which enters the lake on the eastern end, is navigable by canoe. The broad, shallow lake can become rough in a stiff wind.

UL BEND

Jim Wells Creek-East Ridge

Round trip: 15 miles. Hiking time: 2 days. Elevation gain: 450 feet. High point: 2,700 feet. Best time: April through June. USGS maps: Locke Ranch, Mickey Butte, Germaine Coulee East, Germaine Coulee West.

A relatively easy hike along the rolling length of UL Bend. Begin at the end of Road 319, reached from Zortman by driving east on the Dry Fork Road, south on Road 212, and east on Road 201. There are no marked trails in the wilderness, but the terrain makes cross-country travel easy. Old wheel ruts, a legacy of the days before wilderness regulations restricted vehicle travel, lead into the area, passing through the middle of one of several large prairie dog towns found in the UL Bend. Cross Jim Wells Creek, and head southeast toward a low saddle on the eastern ridge. An informal trail winds along the ridge, offering panoramic views of Fort Peck Lake and the Missouri River Breaks on the way to the tip of the peninsula. Make the trip in early morning or late afternoon to avoid the heat and increase the chances of seeing wildlife. There is little water along the route. Water from the lake is muddy but potable if boiled. Picturesque prairie campsites abound, and firewood is plentiful along the lakeshore. Wildfire is always a danger in dry weather, so keep fires small, and extinguish them completely. Also watch for rattlesnakes, which are fairly common in UL Bend.

Crooked Creek to UL Bend

Round trip: 6 miles. Travel time: 4-8 hours. Elevation: 2,250 feet. Best time: April through June. USGS maps: Germaine Coulee East, Germaine Coulee West.

A way to see UL Bend much the same way that Lewis and Clark did. From Bohemian Corner, north of Grassrange on Highway 191, take the Valentine Road to Drag Ridge Trail and Crooked Creek Recreation Area. The trip begins at the mouth of the Musselshell River, near the spot where Lewis and Clark camped May 21, 1805. Paddle northward out of Musselshell Bay, then across Fort Peck Lake to the southern tip of UL Bend. Watch for the sometimes-tricky currents where the Musselshell meets the lake. Fort Peck Lake is an expansive body of water easily whipped into a heavy chop by a light breeze. Windy weather can make the crossing difficult or dangerous. Look along the UL Bend's shore for fossils—which must be left where they are found—or hike up the steep, short slope to explore the area's prairie interior.

MEDICINE LAKE

Sand Hills

Round trip: 2 miles. Hiking time: 1-3 hours. Elevation gain: 150 feet. High point: 2,100 feet. Best time: April through October. USGS maps: Homestead, Medicine Lake, Capneys Lake.

A short, easy stroll across one of the state's most unusual geological features. Drive to the refuge headquarters, 2.5 miles east of the town of Medicine Lake, which is south of Plentywood on Highway 16. Take the dirt patrol road to the southeastern end of Medicine Lake. The Sand Hills are across the barbed wire fence to the south. There are no marked trails, but numerous deer trails criss-cross the rolling terrain. A mile-long walk reaches a series of low sand dunes in the middle of the area. In April and May, ask the refuge manager where to go at dawn to see sharp-tail grouse perform their mating dance.

For additional information, contact the Red Rock Lakes National Wildlife Refuge, Monida Star Route, Box 15, Lima, MT 59739, (406) 276-3347; UL Bend National Wildlife Refuge, in care of Charles M. Russell National Wildlife Refuge, P.O. Box 110, Lewistown, MT 59457, (406) 538-8706. Medicine Lake National Wildlife Refuge, Medicine Lake, MT 59247, (406) 789-2305.

EPILOGUE

Montanans must decide how much wilderness is enough for one generation to pass on to its heirs

How much wilderness is enough? When is a wilderness not a wilderness? Tough questions such as these frame the debate over Montana's last wild lands, a public debate that is far from over. It is a battle of acreages and statistics that is often bewildering even to the participants. It is a controversy in which the basic issues easily become confused.

The statistics of the battle shift as skirmishes over individual areas are won and lost. But in broad brush, they sketch a profile of the struggle. A century ago, virtually all of Montana's 93 million acres were wild. Today, 82 million acres are developed or devoted to resource production—nearly 88 percent of the state. Of the roughly 11.3 million acres that remain wild, only 3.4 million have been set aside by Congress as wilderness. Another 1.1 million are undeveloped lands within national parks and recreation areas. That leaves 6.8 million acres of wild land that is not wilderness and may not remain wild for long. The battle lines that are already drawn make it clear that the greatest share of it is destined to be opened to resource development.

Nearly one-third of Montana, 27.6 million acres, is federal land managed mostly by the Forest Service. In 1978, that agency took an inventory of its remaining wild lands and found that 5.7 of its 16.7 million acres were potentially suitable for wilderness designation. The Bureau of Land Management, in a similar 1979 inventory, found that 2.2 of its 6.3 million acres in Montana were still roadless. Since then, both agencies have recommended that most remaining wild lands be opened to production-oriented resource management. The Forest Service recommended preservation of only one-tenth of what is left, while the BLM

has released all but about 400,000 acres from wilderness consideration.

Conservationists have acceded to the development of more than half the roadless acreage, but they are seeking wilderness designation for slightly less than 2 million acres of Forest Service land. Their proposal, dubbed Alternative W, would double the size of the state's wilderness system. But even if the number of designated wilderness areas increases, the actual amount of wild land in Montana is sure to diminish as new roads are punched into those lands released for development.

On one level, the wilderness debate is a confrontation between different visions of what Montana is today and what it might be in the future. Many in the conservation movement consider the mining and timber industries' past to be a mixture of good and bad and their future to be an uncertainty. Watching newcomers move to Montana in search of wild lands and a clean environment, they conclude that wilderness will be of great importance as the state's recreation industry develops. Outfitter Smoke Elser of Missoula believes Montana and the Pacific Northwest are poised on the edge of an unprecedented boom in the recreation industry. Others believe recreation could be a long-term growth industry that would help stabilize the economic ups and downs of the timber and mining industries.

Opposing interests view the state's traditional basic industries—agriculture, timber, livestock, and mineral development—as the best hope for the future. "The idea that we have to lock up our natural resources and not have the opportunity to develop them is really detrimental to our society," says Mike Micone of the Western Environmental Trade Association, an organization that speaks for a broad cross section of Montana industries on resource issues. Although he acknowledges the need for some wilderness, Micone believes that wilderness blocks the multiple use of public lands by prohibiting most uses.

Laws governing the Forest Service make it clear that wilderness is

High limestone cliffs keep Refrigerator Canyon, east of Helena, cool even on the hottest days. The canyon is part of a proposed 10,000-acre addition to the Gates of the Mountains Wilderness. Montana has more than 6 million acres of wild, but unprotected, land.

compatible with the multiple-use philosophy. But to people like Micone, multiple use means more than the passive production of water, wildlife, fish, and forage by natural processes. It implies active use: resource development; control of weeds, forest insects, and disease; and harvesting of timber before it dies and rots. It implies extraction of minerals—commodities that are not renewable—to satisfy the needs and demands of the present age. Wilderness forbids access by roads and mechanized equipment. Resources such as water, wood, livestock forage, fish, and wildlife may be used, but not in a way that conspicuously alters the appearance of the land or the processes of nature. By contrast, outside the wilderness man can manipulate the forests or alter the land with heavy equipment and chemicals to increase production of resources or to favor one resource over another.

The wilderness issue is especially thorny for the timber industry, whose leaders want to know how much forest land will be available for lumber production in the future. Before the Wilderness Act of 1964, it appeared that nearly all would be available. Wilderness preservation has changed the outlook, as has a decade of national forest planning. Forest plans have revealed soil and watershed limits or wildlife needs that spell further reductions in timber yields. At the same time that prospects for logging have dimmed for marginal and roadless lands, the costs of road construction and production on such lands have mounted. These changes cloud the future for an industry already battered by recession and beset by competition from more productive forests in the Northwest and Southeast.

Conservationists complain that timber management on roadless lands is becoming a drain on the taxpayer instead of a profitable enterprise returning money to the federal treasury. Ed Madej, president of the Montana Wilderness Association, notes that in fiscal year 1983, Montana's ten national forests lost $30 million on timber that sold for less than it cost to harvest it. Madej and others question whether it makes economic sense to grow new trees commercially on marginal lands. Instead, they say, the region should concentrate on more intensive timber management on only the most productive lands.

Foresters point out that timber must be harvested when and where it is mature, at least until the virgin forests with their varied-aged timber stands have been converted to an even production schedule. Miners say that minerals must be taken where they are found. The jobs and taxes from the timber and mining industries have, at least so far, meant much more to the state's economy than those in the recreation industry.

Wilderness critics complain about the waste of raw materials and loss of jobs in basic industry that result when wilderness areas are designated. Conservationists denounce the environmental damage, erosion, reforestation problems, and visual damage that have resulted from poor logging and mining practices of the past.

In the end, conservation leaders like Bill Cunningham of the Montana Wilderness Association return to the theme that wild lands are being lost, not increased. Wilderness is a shrinking pool, and the idea that more wild land can be created by congressional act is ludicrous, he says. Debate about adding new wilderness areas simply muddles the fact that many of Montana's wild areas are steadily being developed. Since the Forest Service inventory of wild lands in 1979, the agency has built roads and laid out timber sales on nearly 575,000 wildland acres—more land than it recommended for further wilderness study.

The contention over the last remaining wild areas will undoubtedly be but a footnote in history, but it is a benchmark in American progress that should not pass without a long moment of reflection. Wilderness is a link to the past and to the wild species that are our fellow travelers on this planet. It represents knowledge yet untapped, possibilities untried, resources undiscovered. How much should any one generation consume? How much wilderness is enough for one generation to pass on to its heirs? Should the present generation make the final wilderness allocations? Will they remain final even if they are made? The debate raises questions that can be answered with certainty only by future generations—people who will look back either with wonder and scorn at the profligacy of their forebears or with admiration and gratitude to an age of vision.

Skiers traverse a slope near Heart Lake, south of western Montana's Hoodoo Pass. The area, which bears indelible marks of the great 1910 fire, is part of a proposed wilderness.

About the Authors

Carl Davaz

Don Schwennesen

Steve Woodruff

Carl Davaz, 31, grew up in a military family and has traveled throughout the United States, the Far East, Europe, and Central America. He was taught to appreciate wilderness and first experienced it as a boy in Alaska. He began his career as a photographer on the staff of the Topeka, Kansas, *Capital-Journal.* In 1978, he received a letter from a brother describing the grandeur of the Bob Marshall Wilderness and its magnificent Chinese Wall. A year later, Davaz became the *Missoulian's* director of photography, and in 1980, on his first extended Montana backcountry trip, he stood in awe of the Chinese Wall. In a single year, he explored and photographed each of Montana's 15 wilderness areas, making nine trips into his favorite, the Bob Marshall. His photographs have appeared in publications such as *Time, Sports Illustrated, Business Week,* and *The New York Times.* He lives in Missoula with his wife, Kim, and daughters, Elsa and Claire.

Don Schwennesen, 42, has a deep interest in conservation that has been nurtured through travels on four continents. Born in Chicago, he spent his youth in suburban Philadelphia and graduated from Trinity College in Hartford, Connecticut, where he also held his first newspaper job, with the Hartford *Courant.* His outdoor experiences have taken him across much of America and from Norway to North Africa. He prepared the chapters on the Bob Marshall, Scapegoat, Great Bear, Cabinet Mountains, Mission Mountains, Gates of the Mountains, Welcome Creek, and Anaconda-Pintler wilderness areas. A Montana resident since 1970, he is a *Missoulian* writer covering a region that includes both the Bob Marshall and Glacier National Park. He lives near Flathead Lake with his wife, Rose, and children, Don, Dan, and Heidi, where the family hikes, skis, grows organic cherries, tends sheep, and converts an old cottage to a passive solar home.

Steve Woodruff, 28, writes about natural resources and the environment for the *Missoulian.* "Too many people think of wilderness as a recreation issue," he says. "In fact, it is the ultimate environmental issue, involving some of the most important land-use decisions of our generation." Born in upstate New York and reared near Seattle, he began exploring the wilds of western Montana as a young boy. Woodruff graduated in 1978 from Washington State University, where he studied journalism and forestry, and worked on newspapers in Oregon and Washington before moving to Montana in 1982. He visited 11 Montana wilderness areas and wrote the chapters on the Absaroka-Beartooth, Selway-Bitterroot, Lee Metcalf, Rattlesnake, Red Rock Lakes, UL Bend, and Medicine Lake wilderness areas. He and his wife, Carol, who is a writer and an artist, live in Missoula with their yellow Labrador retriever, Emily du Claw.

Acknowledgments

The authors are grateful to the people, organizations, and agencies named in the text, as well as to the following people for their generous assistance: John Balla, Bud Baumann, Tom Brown, Cass Chinske, Bill Cunningham, Jim Dolan, Barbara Funk, Jerry Holloron, Brad Hurd, Payson Lowell, Herschal Mays, Fred Matt, Jim McCollum, Terry and Karen McEneaney, Bud and Janet Moore, Joe Mussulman, Bob Mutch, Lloyd Reesman, Sue Root, Roger Stang, Peter Stark, Jerry Stokes, Darwon Stoneman, Gene Stroops, Bob Twist, and the entire staff of the *Missoulian.*

Special thanks to Kim Davaz, Rose Schwennesen, and Carol Susan Woodruff, whose support and understanding made this book possible.